Completely FREE Colleges

Jennifer Cook - DeRosa

DEDICATION

To my sweet husband.

CONTENTS

ACKNOWLEDGMENTS

This book couldn't have made it to press without the help of my editors, proof-readers, and researchers. You guys are great!

Falyn Crawford, Sherri Crawford, Courtney Brooke Fogie, Seth Fogie, Sarah Frisk, Jorge Guzman, Carol Hicks, Julie Jumes, Dena Marie Keene, Adeline Moore, Danielle Moore, Christine Murray, Ali Ophoven, Tracy Ophoven, Augusto Ortiz de Villate, Alison Romeo, Mary Wright, Laura Zielke, and Zachary Zielke

1 GETTING STARTED

"A pessimist sees the difficulty in every opportunity;
an optimist sees the opportunity in every difficulty."
-Winston Churchill

I love finding a deal. While researching my first book, *Homeschooling for College Credit*, I stumbled upon special programs that provided free college tuition for high school students. Later, while plowing through the U.S. Department of Education's database of 39,000 accredited college programs, I started to notice many colleges could be tuition-free in specific circumstances. In other words, if you were willing to move to another city, work for a specific company, met income criteria, or study a certain major, your tuition could be waived. Unfortunately for the students, this information isn't really advertised. I began collecting and organizing every possible way a student could attend college without paying cash, and it became the foundation for my work on this book, *Completely FREE Colleges*.

What do I mean by free? My definition of "free" means 100% free tuition. Every college scenario in this book meets that definition. You may have to pay in time or service, but you won't pay cash. Now, no matter where you spend the next few years, you'll have living expenses, and living expenses aren't free. Your living expenses are a variable beyond the scope of this book, however, a frugal student with a part time job during the school year and full time work during the summer can cover modest living expenses and graduate without student loan debt. A few programs we'll look at even cover the student's living expenses, but that's the exception, not the rule. I anticipate the reader of this book is probably already frugal, but the costs associated with maintaining your lifestyle are up to you. What I'm going to help you tackle is the one cost most people pay full price for: tuition.

What kind of tuition? There are two types of tuition costs, credit and non-credit. Non-credit tuition doesn't result in a degree. Free adult education courses, professional development, MOOCS, and huge open education initiatives through edX or Khan Academy are wonderful, but since they won't count toward a full degree, we won't explore those options in this book. For this book, I've only included options that result in a full degree; either an associate's (2 year) or bachelor's (4 year) degree. There is one exception, which you'll find in the chapter for senior citizens.

So, who pays my bill? It depends. Tuition costs will either be covered up front, or reimbursed to you upon completion. Chapters 1-10 explore "no cash up front" options, while chapters 11 and 12 are "reimbursement" programs.

What about scholarships? There are a handful of fantastic scholarship programs for the 2016 academic year (see chapter 10). Most scholarships, however, are not fantastic. Most scholarships give you the illusion of saving money and are nothing more than marketing tools to drive enrollment, or token awards given by local community groups. A student who receives a $500 or $1000 scholarship, but chooses to attend a college they can't afford, will repay their "scholarship" dozens of times over in student loan interest. Don't step over dollars to save pennies.

Will you tell me how to go to (my college) for free?
Unfortunately, no. Flexibility is your friend. You can check the back index in the back of this book to see if a specific college is listed.

This can't be true, nothing is ever free. Clearly, *someone* is paying your tuition. The focus of this book is to find the scenarios in which *you* won't have to pay your tuition. On occasion, businesses supply grants to help generate a skilled workforce, establish training programs in fields where a severe shortage can hurt an essential segment of industry, or simply to repopulate a community. Some cities have instituted programs for their residents. For private schools, large endowments and private donations of wealthy alumni help fund scholarships and tuition-free programs. Most of the colleges in this book also participate in the title IV financial aid program, so in cases where unfunded expenses exist (ex. textbooks, meals, dorms or rent) a student can use cash from working, grants, and scholarship to cover the difference.

What about deaf or blind students? Most public colleges and universities in the United States will waive tuition for students who are legally blind or deaf. If you live in Texas, it's the law! If you are blind or deaf, be sure to investigate free tuition waivers in your state before chasing down scholarships and loans.

In summary, there are many ways you can earn a college degree for free, but your talents, goals, and dedication will determine which options make sense for you. We'll dissect each of these strategies as we go. Have no fear, there are many ways for the resourceful student to earn their degree tuition-free!

Helpful Terms

ACT: American College Testing. Visit www.actstudent.org for more information.

AP: Advanced Placement Test. High school students achieving certain scores may be eligible for advanced standing or college credit from their college. Visit www.collegeboard.org for more information.*

CLEP: College Level Exam Program. Open to all ages, students achieving a certain score may be eligible for college credit. Visit www.collegeboard.org for more information.*

Distance learning: Instruction that does not require the physical presence of the student. Distance learning can be synchronous (all students viewing streamed content at the same time) or asynchronous (student view pre-recorded lectures or studies on their own).

Dual enrollment: When a high school student is enrolled in one class, but earning credit at two schools for their work. In most cases, the two schools are your high school (or homeschool) and a local college.

Graduate degree: A master's or doctorate degree.

National Accreditation: Not to be confused with regional accreditation, colleges that have national accreditation are generally non-traditional programs, faith-based institutions, or career schools. Credits earned at a nationally accredited college don't usually transfer "up" into a regionally accredited colleges, or qualify toward licensed professions (teacher, doctor, nurse, etc.). NA colleges are considered acceptable in many fields, including trade or religious occupations.

Open Enrollment: Non-competitive college admissions. Any student meeting the entrance requirements may enroll. Community colleges are open enrollment colleges.

Regional Accreditation: Considered the gold standard. Regionally accredited colleges readily transfer credits between each other and participate in federal financial aid programs. Regionally accredited degrees are required for most state-governed licenses (teacher, doctor, nurse, etc.). If a college you are considering is not regionally accredited, be sure to understand the limitations of that deficiency. All colleges in this book are regionally accredited unless otherwise noted.

SAT: Student Aptitude Test. Visit www.collegeboard.org for more information.

Tuition: The cost charged by a college for a course. Tuition fees are typically based on a "per credit" system. A course that is 3 credit hours would cost the rate of tuition times three.

Undergraduate degree: An associate's or bachelor's degree. "Under" the graduate level of study.

*For help using "credit by exam" strategies, check out my first book, *Homeschooling for College Credit*.

Jennifer Cook - DeRosa

2 FREE TUITION FOR EVERYONE

"Outstanding people have one thing in common:
An absolute sense of mission."
-Zig Ziglar

What's better than free? Believe it or not, some colleges have generous donations and huge endowments committed to keeping the cost of education to the absolute minimum. If you're fortunate enough to gain admittance, the following colleges in this chapter waive 100% of tuition costs for all admitted students. In some cases, the student may qualify for grants or scholarships to pay additional costs like books, transportation, meals, or dormitories. As expected, admission to these colleges is competitive to extremely competitive. There are a handful of colleges that used to waive 100% of tuition, but have discontinued their program. I'll include these colleges for your reference since you'll still find them included on old lists.

Barclay College

607 Kingman Ave., Havilland, KS 67059

(800) 862-0226

www.barclaycollege.edu

Type: Private Religious College

Accreditation: Pre-accredited, not regionally accredited

Religious affiliation: Christian, affiliated

U.S. News & World Report National Rank: Unranked

Regular admissions: SAT or ACT required. 2 letters of recommendation and phone interview.

Homeschool admissions: No difference

SAT requirement: 500 minimum or 12 graded transfer credits

ACT requirement: 18 minimum or 12 graded transfer credits

Acceptance rate: 100%

Acceptance category: Open enrollment

CLEP acceptance policy: 32 exams are credit-eligible

AP acceptance policy: Undisclosed

Transfer credit acceptance policy: Transfer credit held until 30 credits are completed in residence

Housing: Yes

Co-ed housing: No

Athletic programs: Yes

Free undergraduate options: Campus based associate and Bachelor's degrees, 15 majors

Free distance learning: No

What's free? 100% tuition, campus based degrees

What's not? Living expenses, books, and dorm. Dorm/meal plan fee $12,000 per year.

Eligibility: 100% of accepted students

Service requirement: None

College of the Ozarks

PO Box 17, Point Lookout, MO 65726

(417) 334-6411

www.ozarks.edu

Type: Private Liberal Arts

Accreditation: Regional

Religious affiliation: Christian

U.S. News & World Report National Rank: #4 (Regional Colleges, Midwest) #1 (Best Undergraduate Teaching)

Regular admissions: Strong preference given to applicants from the region and demonstrated financial need. Students of alumni are given preference.

Homeschool admissions: No difference

SAT requirement: >950

ACT requirement: >20

Acceptance rate: 9%

Acceptance category: Elite/exceptionally competitive

CLEP acceptance policy: 23 exams are credit-eligible, 30 credit maximum allowance

AP acceptance policy: Any exam score of 4 or better

Transfer credit acceptance policy: An Associate of Arts degree from a regionally accredited college will fill general education requirements. A cap of 5 dual-enrolled courses may be accepted.

Housing: Required

Co-ed housing: No

Athletic programs: Yes

Free undergraduate options: Campus Bachelor's only, 42 majors

Free distance learning: No

What's free? Tuition

What's not? Living expenses, books, and dorm. Dorm/meal plan $6,500 per year.

Eligibility: 100% of accepted students are eligible

Service requirement: 15-hours per week plus two 40-hour weeks

Cooper Union for the Advancement of Science and Art

30 Cooper Sq., New York, NY 10003
(212) 353-4100
www.cooper.edu
Type: Private Arts and Sciences
Accreditation: Regional
Religious affiliation: No
U.S. News & World Report National Rank: #2 (Regional)

UPDATE: Cooper Union used to offer full tuition scholarships for all students. The college discontinued this program in 2013

Curtis Institute of Music

1726 Locust St., Philadelphia, PA 19103

(215) 893-5252

www.curtis.edu

Type: Private Performing Arts College

Accreditation: Regional

Religious affiliation: No

U.S. News & World Report National Rank: Unranked

Regular admissions: Audition and SAT scores

Homeschool admissions: No difference

SAT requirement: Yes

ACT requirement: No

Acceptance rate: 5%

Acceptance category: Elite/exceptionally competitive

CLEP acceptance policy: No

AP acceptance policy: Credit for a score 4 or better

Transfer credit acceptance policy: No

Housing: Yes

Co-ed housing: Yes

Athletic programs: No

Free undergraduate options: Campus Bachelor's or masters, 12 majors

Free distance learning: No

What's free? 100% tuition

What's not? Living expenses, books, and dorm

Eligibility: 100% of students receive free tuition. Income eligibility for living expenses

Service requirement: Music lab/orchestra

Deep Springs College

Deep Springs Ranch Rd., Highway 168, Big Pine, CA 89010
(760) 872-2000
www.deepsprings.edu
Type: Private Junior College (males under age 25 only)
Accreditation: Regional
Religious affiliation: No
U.S. News & World Report National Rank: Unranked
Regular admissions: 2-stage application process. Stage 1 requires SAT or ACT and 3 essays. Stage 2 applicants submit additional essays and letters of reference
Homeschool admissions: No difference
SAT requirement: upper 700's
ACT requirement: upper 30's
Acceptance rate: 5-15% (11 to 15 students accepted yearly)
Acceptance category: Competitive to exceptionally competitive
CLEP acceptance policy: No
AP acceptance policy: No
Transfer credit acceptance policy: Not accepted
Housing: Yes
Co-ed housing: No
Athletic programs: No
Free undergraduate options: Campus Associates of Arts degree optional
Free distance learning: No
What's free? 100% tuition, room, board, and meal plan
What's not? Books
Eligibility: 100% of accepted students
Service requirement: Labor is a pillar of the program. All students work 20 hours per week in service to the college's orchard, garden, farm, or cattle ranch.

Franklin W. Olin College of Engineering

Olin Way, Needham, MA 02492

(781) 292-2300

www.olin.edu

Type: Private Engineering College

Accreditation: Regional

Religious affiliation: No

U.S. News & World Report National Rank: #3 (Undergraduate Engineering)

UPDATE: Olin College used to offer full tuition scholarships for all students. The college discontinued this program in 2009, however still awards 50% tuition scholarships to all students.

St. Louis Christian College

1360 Grandview Dr., Florissant, MO 63033

(314) 837-6777

www.stlchristian.edu

Type: Private Religious College

Accreditation: Not regionally accredited

Religious affiliation: Christian, affiliated

U.S. News & World Report National Rank: Unranked

UPDATE: St. Louis/St. Louis Christian College used to offer full tuition scholarships for all students living on campus. The college discontinued this program in 2013.

United States Air Force Academy

HQ USAFA/RRS, 2304 Cadet Dr., USAF Academy, CO 80840

(800) 443-9266

www.usafa.af.mil

Type: Military Academy

Accreditation: Regional

Religious affiliation: No

U.S. News & World Report National Rank: #27 (National) #5 (Undergraduate Engineering) #62 (Undergraduate Business)

Regular admissions: At least 17 but not 23 years of age, unmarried, no dependents, SAT or ACT, interview, High School Diploma or GED. Applicant must also obtain nomination from a U.S. Senator or U.S. Representative, the Vice President of the U.S., the President of the United States, or other specialized category.

Homeschool admissions: Full criteria outlined in "Advice to Homeschool Applicants" Air Force booklet.

SAT requirement: mid to high 600's

ACT requirement: 30

Acceptance rate: 15.4%

Acceptance category: Competitive

CLEP acceptance policy: No

AP acceptance policy: Score of 4 or more

Transfer credit acceptance policy: Considered

Housing: Yes

Co-ed housing: Yes

Athletic programs: Yes

Free undergraduate options: Campus Bachelor's only, 27 majors

Free distance learning: No

What's free? 100% tuition, room, board, meal plan, and books. Cadets earn monthly pay.

What's not? NA

Eligibility: All students

Service requirement: Upon graduation, serve as a commissioned officer in the Air Force for at least 8 years. 10 years for pilots.

United States Coast Guard Academy

31 Mohegan Ave., New London, CT 06320

(800) 883-8724

www.cga.edu

Type: Military Academy

Accreditation: Regional

Religious affiliation: No

U.S. News & World Report National Rank: #1 (Regional) #12 (Undergraduate Engineering)

Regular admissions: At least 17 but not 23 years of age, SAT or ACT, High School Diploma or GED. Physical health and fitness standards required. Special nomination is not required.

Homeschool admissions: No difference, community college coursework suggested

SAT requirement: No minimum. >1100 combined suggested

ACT requirement: No minimum. >24 suggested

Acceptance rate: 16.5%

Acceptance category: Competitive

CLEP acceptance policy: No

AP acceptance policy: No

Transfer credit acceptance policy: Yes. Credit granted does not reduce length of curriculum

Housing: Yes

Co-ed housing: Yes

Athletic programs: Yes

Free undergraduate options: Campus Bachelor's only, 13 majors

Free distance learning: No

What's free? 100% tuition, room, board, meal plan, and books. Cadets earn monthly pay.

What's not? NA

Eligibility: All students

Service requirement: Upon graduation, commissioned ensigns are obligated to serve at least 5 years.

United States Merchant Marine Academy

300 Steamboat Rd., Great Neck, NY 11024

(516) 773-5258

www.usmma.edu

Type: Military Academy

Accreditation: Regional

Religious affiliation: No

U.S. News & World Report National Rank: #3 (Regional) #29 (Undergraduate Engineering)

Regular admissions: At least 17 but not 23 years of age, unmarried, no dependents, SAT or ACT, interview, High School Diploma or GED. Applicant must also obtain nomination from a U.S. Senator or U.S. Representative from the applicant's state of residence. Physical health and fitness standards required.

Homeschool admissions: No difference

SAT requirement: >560

ACT requirement: >24

Acceptance rate: 18.2%

Acceptance category: Competitive

CLEP acceptance policy: No

AP acceptance policy: No

Transfer credit acceptance policy: No

Housing: Yes

Co-ed housing: Yes

Athletic programs: Yes

Free undergraduate options: Campus Bachelor's only, 5 majors

Free distance learning: No

What's free? 100% tuition, room, board, meal plan, and books

What's not? NA

Eligibility: All students

Service requirement: Graduates can choose to work 5 years in the U.S. maritime industry with 8 years of service as an officer in any reserve unit of the armed forces or 5 years active duty in any of the nation's armed forces.

United States Military Academy
West Point, NY
(845) 938-4011
www.usma.edu
Type: Military Academy
Accreditation: Regional
Religious affiliation: No
U.S. News & World Report National Rank: #24 (National)
Regular admissions: At least 17 but not 22 years of age, unmarried, no dependents, SAT or ACT, interview, High School Diploma or GED. Applicant must also obtain nomination from a U.S. Senator or U.S. Representative, the Vice President of the U.S., or the President of the United States. Fitness standards required.
Homeschool admissions: No difference
SAT requirement: >600
ACT requirement: >25
Acceptance rate: 9%
Acceptance category: Elite/exceptionally competitive
CLEP acceptance policy: No
AP acceptance policy: No
Transfer credit acceptance policy: No
Housing: Yes
Co-ed housing: Yes
Athletic programs: Yes
Free undergraduate options: Campus Bachelor's only, 36 majors
Free distance learning: No
What's free? 100% tuition, room, board, meal plan, and books. Cadets earn monthly pay.
What's not? NA
Eligibility: All students
Service requirement: Upon graduation, you will be commissioned as a second lieutenant in the Army and serve for five years on active duty (if you choose to depart the Army after five years, you will be required to serve three years in the Inactive Ready Reserve).

United States Naval Academy

121 Blake Rd., Annapolis, MD 21402

(410) 293-1000

www.usna.edu

Type: Military Academy

Accreditation: Regional

Religious affiliation: No

U.S. News & World Report National Rank: #13 (National) #6 (Undergraduate Engineering)

Regular admissions: At least 17 but not 23 years of age, unmarried, no dependents, SAT or ACT, interview, High School Diploma or GED. Applicant must also obtain nomination from a U.S. Senator or U.S. Representative, the Vice President of the U.S., or the President of the United States. Physical health and fitness standards required.

Homeschool admissions: Detailed curriculum descriptions required

SAT requirement: mid 600's

ACT requirement: high 20's

Acceptance rate: 7.4%

Acceptance category: Elite/exceptionally competitive

CLEP acceptance policy: No

AP acceptance policy: Score of 4 or more

Transfer credit acceptance policy: No

Housing: Yes

Co-ed housing: Yes

Athletic programs: Yes

Free undergraduate options: Campus Bachelor's only, 26 majors

Free distance learning: No

What's free? 100% tuition, room, board, meal plan, and books. Cadets earn monthly pay.

What's not? NA

Eligibility: All students

Service requirement: 5 years active duty service required.

Webb Institute

298 Crescent Beach Rd., Glen Cove, NY 11542

(516) 671-2213

www.webb.edu

Type: Private Engineering College

Accreditation: Regional

Religious affiliation: No

U.S. News & World Report National Rank: #63 (Undergraduate Engineering)

Regular admissions: SAT or ACT, SAT II, specific high school curriculum including calculus. Physical health and fitness standards required.

Homeschool admissions: No difference

SAT requirement: mid to high 600's

ACT requirement: high 20's

Acceptance rate: 29.5%

Acceptance category: Competitive

CLEP acceptance policy: No

AP acceptance policy: No

Transfer credit acceptance policy: No

Housing: Yes

Co-ed housing: No

Athletic programs: Yes

Free undergraduate options: Campus Bachelor's only, 1 major Naval Architecture and Marine Engineering

Free distance learning: No

What's free? 100% tuition

What's not? Room and board $14,500

Eligibility: All students

Service requirement: No

Williamson Free School of Mechanical Trades
106 S. New Middletown Rd., Media, PA 19063
(610) 566-1776
www.williamson.edu
Type: Private Junior College (males only)
Accreditation: Not regionally accredited. Accrediting Commission of Career Schools and Colleges
Religious affiliation: Christian
U.S. News & World Report National Rank: Unranked
Regular admissions: Single males without children not yet 20 years old. High School diploma or GED required. Letters of reference optional.
Homeschool admissions: No difference
SAT requirement: No, but ASVAB test is required
ACT requirement: No
Acceptance rate: 25%
Acceptance category: Competitive
CLEP acceptance policy: No
AP acceptance policy: No
Transfer credit acceptance policy: No
Housing: Yes
Co-ed housing: No
Athletic programs: Yes
Free undergraduate options: Campus diploma or associate degree. 6 majors
Free distance learning: No
What's free? 100% tuition, room, board, meal plan, and books
What's not? Tools
Eligibility: All students
Service requirement: Classes integrate service opportunities in the curriculum

3 FREE TUITION BY GEOGRAPHY

"When I was a kid my parents moved a lot, but I always found them."
-Rodney Dangerfield

It's possible, that choosing where to live based on college scholarship opportunities may seem a little extreme, but many cities are hoping you'll do just that. State and privately funded full tuition programs are popping up faster than I can get them onto this list. To be clear, these are not scholarships you have to win, these are scholarship awards guaranteed to anyone living in the geographic location for a specific length of time.

The following schools provide 100% tuition coverage to anyone living in the specified geographic area. In some cases, a high school diploma from the town is required, and in rare instances, adults are eligible to return to college as long as 10 years after their high school graduation and take advantage of their tuition benefit. Homeschool eligibility varies. There are a handful of programs in the United States that promise kindergarten and elementary school students guaranteed college funding, but I've decided to omit that set since many of those programs have stopped enrolling new students. However, if you'd like to investigate these options on your own, visit SayYestoEducation.org for more information.

In cases where the program identifies as a "last dollar" award, your eligibility starts after any other scholarship or grant money has been applied to your tuition bill. In other words, you can't receive an over-payment cash refund; unneeded money is relinquished. Be sure to investigate the current school's length of residency requirements before packing up the U-Haul! If your city adds a free tuition program that isn't on this list, I want to hear about it! Send me a message at completelyFREECollege@aol.com.

ARIZONA

Pinal County Promise for the Future Program
www.eldoradopromise.com
Type: 100% Tuition college scholarship for high school students
Acceptance category: Open Enrollment
What's free? 100% tuition for 4 semesters at any Central Arizona college.
Free distance learning: Yes, at any 2- or 4-year regionally accredited college.
Regular admissions / eligibility: Pinal County students must register for the program in 8th grade. If student maintains 2.75 GPA and completes 20 hours of community service, they are guaranteed eligible for the award.
Homeschool: Not eligible

ARKANSAS

Arkadelphia Promise Program
www.arkadelphiapromise.com
Type: 100% Tuition college scholarship for high school students
Acceptance category: Open Enrollment
What's free? All students who graduate from Arkadelphia High School District are guaranteed eligible for 4 years of tuition at the 2- or 4-year regionally accredited college of their choice.
Free distance learning: Yes, at any 2- or 4-year regionally accredited college.
Regular admissions / eligibility: The length of time enrolled in the K-12 system determines the award. A minimum of 3 years enrolled prior to high school graduation is required. Students may apply their award to an out of state college, but the award amount will not exceed the current rate of Arkansas public university tuition.
Homeschool: Not eligible

ARKANSAS

El Dorado Promise Program
www.eldoradopromise.com
Type: 100% Tuition college scholarship for high school students
Acceptance category: Open Enrollment
What's free? All students who graduate from El Dorado School District are guaranteed eligible for 5 years 100% tuition, room, board, meals, books, and expenses at the 2 or 4 year regionally accredited college of their choice.
Free distance learning: Yes, at any 2- or 4-year regionally accredited college.
Regular admissions / eligibility: Effective May 2013, Promise program expansion allows students from neighboring districts to obtain eligibility. The length of time enrolled in the K-12 system determines the award.
Homeschool: Not eligible

Mississippi County Great River Promise
www.anc.edu
Type: 100% Tuition college scholarship for high school students
Acceptance category: Open Enrollment
What's free? 4 semesters (2 years) of tuition at Arkansas Northeastern College.
Free distance learning: Yes, at Northeastern College.
Regular admissions / eligibility: All students who graduate from a Mississippi County public high school with 95% attendance, have no drug or DWI offenses, are guaranteed eligible.
Homeschool: Not eligible

CALIFORNIA

La Cuesta Promise Program

www.venturacollege.edu
Type: 100% Tuition college scholarship for high school students
Acceptance category: Open Enrollment
What's free? 100% tuition and fees at Cuesta College for 1 year.
(NOTE: For 100% tuition, the student should choose from the 1-year certificate or diploma programs. Students who choose a 2-year degree must self-fund their second year)
Free distance learning: Yes, at Cuesta College
Regular admissions / eligibility: Student must have graduated in the spring from San Luis Obispo County high school and enroll immediately in the fall. GED and homeschool students are eligible.
Homeschool: Yes

Richmond Promise

www.richmondpromise.org
Type: 100% Tuition college scholarship for high school students
Acceptance category: To be determined
What's free? Program currently in developmental phase
Free distance learning: To be determined
Regular admissions / eligibility: To be determined. Draft document indicates students must graduate from Contra Costa Unified School District.
Homeschool: Predicted ineligible

CALIFORNIA

Ventura Promise Program

www.venturacollege.edu

Type: 100% Tuition college scholarship for high school students

Acceptance category: Open Enrollment

What's free? 100% tuition and fees at Ventura College for 1 year. (NOTE: For 100% tuition, the student should choose from the 1 year certificate or diploma programs. Students who choose a 2 year degree must self-fund their second year)

Free distance learning: Yes, at Ventura College

Regular admissions / eligibility: Student must have graduated from Ventura County high school or have earned a GED within the past 2 years, and be under the age of 20.

Homeschool: Not eligible

ILLINOIS

Galesburg Promise Program

www.sandburg.edu

Type: 100% Tuition college scholarship for high school students

Acceptance category: Open Enrollment

What's free? 100% tuition and fees at Carl Sandburg College

Free distance learning: Yes, at Carl Sandburg College

Regular admissions / eligibility: Student must live in a qualifying address zone. Students must attend K-12 for at least 3 years to become eligible. The length of time enrolled in the K-12 system determines the award.

Homeschool: Not eligible

ILLINOIS

Peoria Promise Program
www.peoriapromise.org
Type: 100% Tuition college scholarship for high school students
Acceptance category: Open Enrollment
What's free? 100% tuition and fees at Illinois Central College.
Free distance learning: Yes, at Illinois Central College
Regular admissions / eligibility: Student must live in a qualifying address zone for at least 3 years to become guaranteed eligible, graduate from qualifying high school, maintain their residence for the duration of the program, maintain GPA of 2.0, and attend at least 67% of classes.
Homeschool: Not eligible

INDIANA

Hammond College Bound Program
www.collegebound.gohammond.com
Type: 100% Tuition college scholarship for high school students
Acceptance category: Open Enrollment
What's free? 100% tuition and fees at any regionally accredited college or university.
Free distance learning: Yes, at any 2- or 4-year regionally accredited college or university
Regular admissions / eligibility: The length of time enrolled in the K-12 system determines the award. Students who entered the district at 6th grade or earlier are guaranteed eligible for 100% tuition. The parents must maintain their residence in the city of Hammond for the duration of the student's award.
Homeschool: Yes

KENTUCKY

Alice Lloyd College
100 Purpose Road, Pippa Passes, KY 41844
1-888-280-4252
www.alc.edu
Type: Private Liberal Arts College
Accreditation: Regional
Religious affiliation: No
U.S. News & World Report Ranking: #29 (Regional)
Regular admissions: SAT or ACT required. Admissions interview.
Homeschool admissions: No difference
SAT requirement: 830 minimum, >1040 suggested
ACT requirement: 17 minimum, >23 suggested
Acceptance rate: 9.43%
Acceptance category: Elite/exceptionally competitive
CLEP acceptance policy: 23 exams are credit-eligible, 30 credit maximum allowance
AP acceptance policy: Any exam score of 3 or better
Transfer credit acceptance policy: 30 credit minimum required to apply for transfer admissions. 64 community college credits accepted. 90 university credits accepted. Does not accept Prior Learning credits
Housing: Dorms available.
Co-ed housing: No
Athletic programs: Yes
Free undergraduate options: Campus-based bachelors only, 18 majors
Free distance learning: No
What's free? 100% of tuition
What's not? Living expenses, books, and dorm.
Eligibility: Must live inside the designated 108 county region which includes Kentucky, Ohio, Tennessee, Virginia, or West Virginia
Service requirement: 160 hour work-study program required per semester

KENTUCKY

Hopkinsville Rotary Scholars Program

hopkinsvillerotary.com

Type: 100% Tuition college scholarship for high school students

Acceptance category: Open Enrollment

What's free? Guaranteed eligible for 100% tuition at Hopkinsville Community College.

Free distance learning: Yes, at Hopkinsville Community College

Regular admissions / eligibility: Student must graduate from Christian County High School, Hopkinsville High School, Heritage Christian Academy, or University Heights Academy. 2.5 GPA and 95% attendance required.

Homeschool: Yes

MARYLAND

Garrett County Scholarship Program

www.garrettcounty.org

Type: 100% Tuition college scholarship for high school students

Acceptance category: Open Enrollment

What's free? Guaranteed eligible for 100% tuition at Garrett College toward certificate or degree program.

Free distance learning: Yes, at Garrett College

Regular admissions / eligibility: Resident of Garrett County for 2 years. Must have high school diploma or GED. Current dual enrolled high school students also eligible.

Homeschool: Yes

MICHIGAN

Baldwin Promise Program

www.baldwinpromise.org

Type: 100% Tuition college scholarship for high school students

Acceptance category: Open Enrollment

What's free? All students who graduate from Baldwin High School are guaranteed eligible for a $5000 per year tuition scholarship. (100% tuition at any in state Michigan community college). Students must attend Baldwin High School for all 4 years to be eligible. Students may use award toward a more expensive Michigan college if they wish.

Free distance learning: Yes, at any Michigan community college

Regular admissions / eligibility: Students must be enrolled a minimum of 4 years to receive any benefit.

Homeschool: Not eligible

Battle Creek Legacy Program

www.legacyscholars.org

Type: 100% Tuition college scholarship for high school students

Acceptance category: Open Enrollment

What's free? All students who graduate from Battle Creek or Lakeview school districts are eligible for free tuition at Kellogg Community College. Students have 5 years to use their award. Students who entered the district at 6th grade or earlier are guaranteed eligible for 100% tuition.

Free distance learning: Yes, at Kellogg Community College

Regular admissions / eligibility: The length of time enrolled in the K-12 system determines the award.

Homeschool: Not eligible

MICHIGAN

Detroit Chamber Scholarship Program
www.detroitchamber.com
Type: 100% Tuition college scholarship for high school students
Acceptance category: Open Enrollment
What's free? 100% free tuition toward the completion of an associate degree or trade degree one of 5 community colleges. (Henry Ford, Schoolcraft, Macomb, Oakland, or Wayne County community colleges)
Free distance learning: Yes, at a qualifying community college
Regular admissions / eligibility: All students who graduate from a Detroit high school and have lived in Detroit for at least 2 years.
Homeschool: Not eligible

Hazel Park Promise Program
www.hazelparkpromise.com
Type: 100% Tuition college scholarship for high school students and young adults
Acceptance category: Open Enrollment
What's free? All students who graduate from Hazel Park school districts are eligible for free tuition toward a 2-year associate's degree.
Free distance learning: Yes, if part of an associate's degree
Regular admissions / eligibility: Students have until the age of 20 to obtain their high school diploma or GED and qualify for the program. Students must have lived within the Hazel Park District boundary for 4 years.
Homeschool: Not eligible

MICHIGAN

Kalamazoo Promise Program
www.kalamazoopromise.com
Type: 100% Tuition college scholarship for high school students
Acceptance category: Open Enrollment
What's free? Guaranteed eligible for 100% tuition and fees at any Michigan community college or participating university.
Free distance learning: Yes, if on approved list
Regular admissions / eligibility: The length of time enrolled in the K-12 system determines the award. Students must be enrolled a minimum of 4 years to receive any benefit, but students enrolled for the duration of their K-12 education receive 100% tuition award. Minimum 2.0 GPA.
Homeschool: Not eligible

Lansing Promise Program
www.lansingpromise.org
Type: 100% Tuition college scholarship for high school students
Acceptance category: Open Enrollment
What's free? All public or private school student who resides in the Lansing school district boundary is eligible for free tuition at Lansing Community College up to 60 credits (associate's degree) or for the first 60 credits toward a bachelor's degree at Michigan State University.
Free distance learning: Yes, at Lansing Community College or Michigan State University.
Regular admissions / eligibility: Students must be enrolled a minimum of 4 years in a Lansing School District public or private school to be eligible, and use their award within 4 years of high school graduation. Students have until the age of 20 to obtain their high school diploma or GED and qualify for the program
Homeschool: Not eligible

MICHIGAN

Northport Promise Program
www.knorthportpromise.com
Type: 100% Tuition college scholarship for high school students
Acceptance category: Open Enrollment
What's free? Guaranteed eligible for 100% tuition and fees at any Michigan community college or participating university
Free distance learning: Yes, if on approved list
Regular admissions / eligibility: The length of time enrolled in the K-12 system determines the award. Students must be enrolled a minimum of 4 years to receive any benefit, but students enrolled for the duration of their K-12 education receive 100% tuition award. Minimum 2.0 GPA. Community service commitment required.
Homeschool: Not eligible

Pontiac Promise Zone Program
www.pontiacpromisezone.org
Type: 100% Tuition college scholarship for high school students
Acceptance category: Open Enrollment
What's free? 100% tuition and books at a Michigan college toward the completion of an associate's degree or 63 credits, whichever happens first.
Free distance learning: Yes, at any Michigan college
Regular admissions / eligibility: Students living in and graduating from the Pontiac area private or public high school area. The length of time enrolled in the K-12 system determines the award. A student may use the award up to 5 years after graduation.
Homeschool: Not eligible

MICHIGAN

Saginaw Promise Program

www.saginawpromise.org

Type: 100% Tuition college scholarship for high school students

Acceptance category: Open Enrollment

What's free? All students who reside in the Saginaw School District are guaranteed eligible for a $2727 per year tuition scholarship. (*NOTE: This award alone only covers 95% of community college tuition) An $8000 award option exists for students attending a 4-year college, however, that does not cover full tuition at any of the state's 4-year colleges or universities.

Free distance learning: Yes, at any Michigan community college

Regular admissions / eligibility: Students must reside in Saginaw for at least 3 continuous years including 12th grade, and graduate from high school in the district.

Homeschool: Not eligible

NEW YORK

Macaulay Honors College at City University of New York

35 West 67th Street, New York, NY 10023

212-729-2900

www.macaulay.cuny.edu

Type: Public State College

Accreditation: Regional

Religious affiliation: No

U.S. News & World Report National Rank: Unranked
Nationally. Regional rank varies by campus

Regular admissions: SAT or ACT. 2 letters of recommendation,
transcript, essay. First time freshman only.

Homeschool admissions: State issued diploma, GED, or letter
from district superintendent

SAT requirement: >1400 suggested

ACT requirement: >28

Acceptance rate: undisclosed

Acceptance category: competitive

CLEP acceptance policy: No

AP acceptance policy: Yes, but varies by campus

Transfer credit acceptance policy: No

Housing: Varies by campus

Co-ed housing: Varies by campus

Athletic programs: Yes

Free undergraduate options: Campus bachelors only, over 400
majors through 8 campuses

Free distance learning: No

What's free? 100% tuition, laptop computer, study abroad, cultural
events admission.

What's not? Room, board, meal plan, books.

Eligibility: New York City resident

Service requirement: No. (Working heavily discouraged)

NEW YORK

Say Yes Buffalo Program
 www.sayyesbuffalo.org
Type: 100% Tuition college scholarship for high school students
Acceptance category: Open Enrollment
What's free? guaranteed eligibility for 100% tuition reimbursement at any New York community college or participating university, SUNY, CUNY
Free distance learning: Yes, if on approved list
Regular admissions / eligibility: Be a resident of the city of Buffalo. Students must be enrolled a minimum of 4 consecutive years to receive 100% tuition award. The length of time enrolled in the 9-12 high school system determines the award. Families earning over $75,000 per year have reduced award.
Homeschool: Not eligible

Say Yes Syracuse Program
 www.sayyessyracuse.org
Type: 100% Tuition college scholarship for high school students
Acceptance category: Open Enrollment
What's free? guaranteed eligibility for 100% tuition reimbursement at any New York community college or participating university, SUNY, CUNY
Free distance learning: Yes, if on approved list
Regular admissions / eligibility: Be a resident of the city of Syracuse. Students must be enrolled a minimum of 3 years to receive 100% tuition award.
Homeschool: Not eligible

NORTH CAROLINA

Cleveland County Promise Program
www.theclevelandcountypromise.com
Type: 100% Tuition college scholarship for high school students
Acceptance category: Open Enrollment
What's free? This award provides 100% tuition at any in-state or out-of-state accredited college in the country. If students apply their award to an out of state college, but the award amount will not exceed the current rate of the highest North Carolina public university tuition rate.
Free distance learning: Yes
Regular admissions / eligibility: The length of time enrolled in the K-12 system determines the award. Students must be enrolled a minimum of 1 year to receive any benefit, but students enrolled for the duration of their K-12 education receive maximum benefit. 85% school attendance required.
Homeschool: Yes

OKLAHOMA

Tulsa Achieves
www.tulsacc.edu/tulsaachieves
Type: 100% Tuition college scholarship for high school students
Acceptance category: Open Enrollment
What's free? This award provides 100% tuition at Tulsa Community College for 63 credits or 3 years.
Free distance learning: Yes
Regular admissions / eligibility: Every high school graduate in Tulsa County who earns 2.0 GPA
Homeschool: Yes

PENNSYLVANIA

Pittsburg Promise Program
www.pittsburghpromise.com
Type: 100% Tuition college scholarship for high school students
Acceptance category: Open Enrollment
What's free? All students who graduate from any Pittsburg public high school or one of its charter schools are guaranteed eligible for up to $10,000 per year for tuition, room, board, meals, and books for use at any accredited 2- or 4-year college in Pennsylvania. This award provides 100% tuition at any community college. Students may qualify for scholarships or grants to cover additional costs at more expensive colleges.
Free distance learning: No
Regular admissions / eligibility: The length of time enrolled in the K-12 system determines the award. Students must be enrolled a minimum of 4 years to receive any benefit, but students enrolled for the duration of their K-12 education receive maximum benefit. Minimum 2.5 GPA and 90% attendance.
Homeschool: Not eligible

TENNESSEE

Tennessee Promise Program
www.tennesseepromise.gov
Type: 100% Tuition college scholarship for high school students
Acceptance category: Open Enrollment
What's free? All students who graduate from a Tennessee high school may attend any of the state's 2-year community colleges or colleges of applied technology for 2 years. Guaranteed eligible for 100% tuition coverage.
Free distance learning: No
Regular admissions / eligibility: Minimum 2.0 GPA and 8 hours of community service required.
Homeschool: Not eligible

TEXAS

Rusk Tyler Junior College Citizens Promise
www.tjc.edu/ruskpromise
Type: 100% Tuition college scholarship for high school students
Acceptance category: Open Enrollment
What's free? 100% of tuition, fees, books, and housing up to $8000 for two years at Tyler Junior College.
Free distance learning: Yes, at Tyler Junior College
Regular admissions / eligibility: All students who have attended Rusk High School for grades 11 and 12, graduate from Rusk High School, and have a minimum 2.5 GPA are guaranteed eligible.
Homeschool: Not eligible

WEST VIRGINIA

West Virginia Promise Program

www.cfwv.com

Type: 100% Tuition college scholarship for high school students

Acceptance category: Open Enrollment

What's free? All students who graduate from high school in the state of West Virginia are guaranteed eligible for $4,750 per year for 4 semesters at a community college, or 8 semesters at a West Virginia university. (See website for current list of approved schools) The award amount covers 100% of community college tuition at all of the participating schools, and 100% tuition at Martinsburg College in West Virginia. Students may qualify for scholarships or grants to cover additional costs at more expensive colleges.

Free distance learning: Yes, if on approved list

Regular admissions / eligibility: Minimum 3.0 GPA, SAT or ACT scores required.

Homeschool: Eligible upon obtaining General Education Diploma. >2500 score required.

Jennifer Cook - DeRosa

4 FREE TUITION BASED ON INCOME

"The fact of being an underdog changes people in ways that we often fail to appreciate. It opens doors and creates opportunities and enlightens and permits things that might otherwise have seemed unthinkable."
-Malcolm Gladwell

On the sitcom *The Middle*, there was a scene this season when Sue received her financial aid package. Frankie shouted "I knew we were poor enough for you to go to college!" As it turns out, Sue's parents hadn't set up a college fund since things like food, rent, and clothing kept getting in the way. Most middle class families don't have the resources to set aside a hundred thousand dollars for each of their children.

This section discusses how income criteria can help you locate colleges that may waive your tuition, and we'll also discuss some of the federal programs that you may qualify for. I'm sure you want to know how *poor* you really have to be. A few colleges in this section restrict free tuition to families earning under $140,000 per year, while others restrict it to about $60,000. Even still, the number of people in your family, the number of students enrolled in college, and a lot of other criteria must all get plugged into the Free Application for Federal Student Aid before "need-based" decisions can be made, so let's start from the top.

Every student entering college should fill out (or may be required to fill out) the Free Application for Federal Student Aid. The FAFSA is available online, and can be completed very quickly from home. Visit www.FAFSA.ed.gov to begin the process. Each state has a specific filing deadline, but expect it to be around June of the same year you hope to start. In nearly every case, even students who will not be using federal financial aid must still complete this form because it's used as an official determiner of your family's need according to the school you're considering. Even if you apply to many colleges, you'll only have to fill out the form once. Each college's financial office will recalculate your need and award according to the costs associated with their program.

A quick word about need based scholarships and waivers. Need-based aid, like the aid in this section, comes from a number of places. Sometimes, it comes from a rich alumni donor paying it forward, sometimes from a state's elected officials, or sometimes as a federal program attempting to improve educational access for all Americans. You should know that need-based aid is frequently earmarked as a "last-dollar" award.

Last dollar awards don't become available until you've received every other award that you're eligible for; these awards are the "last dollars" to fill your account. For instance, assume your college's tuition is $7,000 per year and you have received a "last dollar" tuition scholarship for $7,000. You'll be required to fill out the FAFSA form to check for federal grant eligibility. If you qualify for a $5,000 Pell Grant, you'll receive those funds first, and the amount of your scholarship will be reduced down to $2,000. Tuition is still covered, but this prevents abuse of the system, since some students may qualify for thousands more than their tuition.

It's necessary to discuss one other aspect of financial aid before we continue, scams. Test prep companies and testing services sell names, email addresses, and data to thousands of dot com companies every year. (Yes, even the ACT and SAT will sell your name). It's highly likely that you'll make your way onto at least one list, which will result in being bombarded by companies hoping to make a quick buck. Legitimate financial aid information is found through the U.S.

Department of Education's Federal Financial Aid website www.studentaid.gov.   Unsolicited financial aid and student loan help may be an attempt to steal your identity and prey on vulnerable families hoping to pay for college. In addition, companies promising you money for college, scholarships, or grants that end in dot com should be avoided or used with extreme caution. Never send money to a company promising you money for college. Real scholarships do not have application fees.

The first grant checked for your eligibility is the Pell Grant. Pell Grants can, in many cases, fund an entire degree.

Pell Grants → Free Community College

What: Federal grant money given to undergraduate students attending an accredited college.

Grant: A grant is a gift, not a loan- does not need to be paid back.

How to apply: Fill out the Free Application for Federal Student Aid. FAFSA formula determines eligibility automatically, no additional applications needed.

Eligibility: Income, family size, expenses, and other factors are calculated through the FAFSA.

How much? For the 2015-2016 school year, max award is $5,775.00

Will I get it all? Probably, unless you are not enrolled full time or for a full school year. Pell awards are often split in half, and paid in 2 installments over the course of an academic year.

Is this a last dollar award? No. In fact, it is a first dollar award. You will receive this money automatically if you qualify, and other awards will be applied after your Pell Grant.

What if my college is cheaper than $5,775 per year? You'll receive a cash refund for the overage.

How long? For 12 semesters, approximately 6 years, or until you've completed a bachelor's degree.

How will I know? After you have completed the FAFSA, your college will receive your data and begin calculating your award amount. Your college's financial aid office will contact you with your award amount.

How does a Pell Grant make my community college free? The full award amount $5,775 divided by 30 credits (full time enrollment for 1 year) will pay 100% of tuition at any college in which the tuition cost is approximately $190.00 or less, which includes for nearly every public community college in the country. For students attending a community college of approximately $100 per credit (the national average), the expected overage amount of $2,775 can be used for textbooks, fees, computers, or living expenses. In addition, community colleges are "open enrollment" colleges, which means no competitive admission!

Jennifer's tip: *If you plan to continue on to a 4-year college, choose your community college and 4-year school at the same time. All community colleges have written agreements, called articulation agreements, with 4-year colleges that guarantee a perfect transfer. You save time and money when you don't have to retake classes that you've lost in transfer!*

Berea College

101 Chestnut St, Berea, KY 40403

(859) 985-3000

www.berea.edu

Type: Private Liberal Arts College

Accreditation: Regional

Religious affiliation: Christian, unaffiliated

U.S. News & World Report National Rank: #69 (National)

Regular admissions: SAT or ACT required. 2 letters of endorsement. Admissions interview.

Homeschool admissions: Homeschool Supplement Form

SAT requirement: 1210 minimum >1240 suggested

ACT requirement: 17 minimum >26 suggested

Acceptance rate: 34.01%

Acceptance category: Competitive

CLEP acceptance policy: 25 exams are credit eligible.

AP acceptance policy: Any exam score of 3 or better

Transfer credit acceptance policy: Limited acceptance. Credits must be <10 years old.

Housing: Yes

Co-ed housing: No

Athletic programs: Yes

Free undergraduate options: Campus based Bachelor's degrees, 28 majors

Free distance learning: No

What's free? 100% of tuition, room, board, meals, laptop computer and books.

What's not? NA

Eligibility: 95% of students will meet full income eligibility. 5% must pay $1,400 per year through additional work study, federal financial aid, or scholarships.

Service requirement: Work-study program required each semester, summer work required.

Brown University
Providence, RI 02912
(401) 863-1000
www.brown.edu
Type: Private Research University. Ivy League
Accreditation: Regional
Religious affiliation: No
U.S. News & World Report National Rank: #16 (National) #6 (Best Undergraduate Teaching) #41 (Undergraduate Engineering)
Regular admissions: Participates in Common Application. SAT or ACT required, letters of recommendation, personal statement, and additional criteria for some majors.
Homeschool admissions: Homeschool question set.
SAT requirement: >1540
ACT requirement: >34
Acceptance rate: 8.50%
Acceptance category: Elite/exceptionally competitive
CLEP acceptance policy: No credit, advanced standing
AP acceptance policy: No credit
Transfer credit acceptance policy: Limited. Transfer credit held until 30 credits are completed in residence
Housing: Required
Co-ed housing: Yes
Athletic programs: Yes
Free undergraduate options: campus bachelors only, 70 majors
Free distance learning: No
What's free? 100% tuition, room, and board, meals, travel, and books.
What's not? NA
Eligibility: Any family earning less than $100,000 per year.
Service requirement: No

Columbia University

2960 Broadway, New York, NY 10027

(212) 854-1754

www.columbia.edu

Type: Private Research University. Ivy League

Accreditation: Regional

Religious affiliation: No

U.S. News & World Report National Rank: #4 (National) #12 (Undergraduate Manufacturing) #22 (Undergraduate Biomedical) #22 (Undergraduate Engineering)

Regular admissions: Participates in Common Application. SAT or ACT required, letters of recommendation, personal statement, and additional criteria for some majors.

Homeschool admissions: Curriculum for all 4 years of high school. Letters from instructors.

SAT requirement: >760

ACT requirement: >32

Acceptance rate: 6.9%

Acceptance category: Elite/exceptionally competitive

CLEP acceptance policy: No credit.

AP acceptance policy: Credit or advanced standing for a score 4 or better

Transfer credit acceptance policy: Limited.

Housing: Yes

Co-ed housing: Yes

Athletic programs: Yes

Free undergraduate options: Campus bachelors only, 80 majors.

Free distance learning: No

What's free? 100% tuition, room, board, meal plan, and books.

What's not? NA

Eligibility: Any family earning less than $60,000 per year

Service requirement: 10 hours per week

Cornell University

Ithaca, NY 14853

(607) 255-2000

www.cornell.edu

Type: Private Research Ivy League

Accreditation: Regional

Religious affiliation: No

U.S. News & World Report National Rank: #15 (National) #11 (Undergraduate Business) #10 (Undergraduate Engineering)

Regular admissions: Participates in Common Application and Universal College Application. SAT or ACT required, letters of recommendation, personal statement, and additional criteria for some majors. Interview required.

Homeschool admissions: No difference

SAT requirement: >640

ACT requirement: >30

Acceptance rate: 15.6%

Acceptance category: Competitive

CLEP acceptance policy: No

AP acceptance policy: Credit for a score 4 or better

Transfer credit acceptance policy: 12 credits required to apply as transfer student.

Housing: Yes

Co-ed housing: Yes

Athletic programs: Yes

Free undergraduate options: Campus bachelors only, 80 majors.

Free distance learning: No

What's free? 100% tuition, room, board, meal plan, and books.

What's not? NA

Eligibility: Families earning less than $60,000 per year.

Service requirement: No

Dartmouth College

6016 McNutt Hall, Hanover, NH 03755

(603) 646-1110

www.dartmouth.edu

Type: Private Research Ivy League

Accreditation: Regional

Religious affiliation: No

U.S. News & World Report National Rank: #11 (National) #48 (Undergraduate Engineering) #4 (Undergraduate Teaching)

Regular admissions: SAT, teacher evaluations, letters of recommendation, essay, and portfolio.

Homeschool admissions: Letters from non-family member teachers and demonstrated language ability through Advanced Placement exam or SAT II

SAT requirement: >735

ACT requirement: >32

Acceptance rate: 10%

Acceptance category: Elite/exceptionally competitive

CLEP acceptance policy: Considered, not guaranteed.

AP acceptance policy: Credit or exemption for score of 5

Transfer credit acceptance policy: Community college or online credit not accepted, up to 4 credits from an accredited 4-year university may be evaluated for transfer.

Housing: Yes

Co-ed housing: Yes

Athletic programs: Yes

Free undergraduate options: Campus bachelors only

Free distance learning: No

What's free? 100% tuition, room, board, meal plan, and books.

What's not? NA

Eligibility: Families earning less than $100,000 per year.

Service requirement: In some cases

Harvard University

86 Brattle Street, Cambridge, MA 02138

(617) 495-1000

www.harvard.edu

Type: Private Research Ivy League

Accreditation: Regional

Religious affiliation: No

U.S. News & World Report National Rank: #2 (National) #26 (Undergraduate Engineering)

Regular admissions: Participates in Common Application and Universal College Application. SAT and SAT II required, letters of recommendation, personal statement, and transcript.

Homeschool admissions: No difference

SAT requirement: mid 700's

ACT requirement: low 30's

Acceptance rate: 5.8%

Acceptance category: Elite/exceptionally competitive

CLEP acceptance policy: No

AP acceptance policy: score of 5 for advanced standing (no credit)

Transfer credit acceptance policy: 16 course transfer maximum. Online, dual enrollment, summer school courses not accepted

Housing: Yes

Co-ed housing: Yes

Athletic programs: Yes

Free undergraduate options: Campus bachelors only, 48 majors

Free distance learning: No

What's free? 100% tuition, room, board, meal plan, and books.

What's not? NA

Eligibility: Families earning less than $65,000 per year

Service requirement: Work-study program required each semester, summer work expected.

Massachusetts Institute of Technology (MIT)

77 Massachusetts Avenue, Cambridge, MA 02139

(617) 253-1000

web.mit.edu

Type: Private Research University

Accreditation: Regional

Religious affiliation: No

U.S. News & World Report National Rank: #7 (National) #2 (Undergraduate Business) #1 (Undergraduate Engineering)

Regular admissions: Essay, ACT or SAT, SAT II math and science required, letters of recommendation from science teacher and language teacher.

Homeschool admissions: Supplemental document cover sheet. Diploma/GED not required. MIT Open Courseware encouraged.

SAT requirement: High 700's. SAT II Subject Math score >770. SAT II Subject Science score >740

ACT requirement: High 30's

Acceptance rate: 7.9%

Acceptance category: Elite/exceptionally competitive

CLEP acceptance policy: No

AP acceptance policy: Credit for scores of 5

Transfer credit acceptance policy: Yes, for students who have completed 1 full year at a regionally accredited college or university.

Housing: Yes

Co-ed housing: Yes

Athletic programs: Yes

Free undergraduate options: Campus bachelors only, 46 majors

Free distance learning: No

What's free? 100% tuition

What's not? Room, board, meal plan, and books may be partially met by scholarship

Eligibility: Families earning less than $75,000

Service requirement: Work-study program may be required

Princeton University

Princeton, NJ 08544

(609) 258-3000

www.princeton.edu

Type: Private Research University. Ivy League

Accreditation: Regional

Religious affiliation: No

U.S. News & World Report National Rank: #1 (National) #1 (Undergraduate Teaching)

Regular admissions: Participates in Common Application and Universal College Application. SAT and SAT II required, letters of recommendation, personal statement, and transcript

Homeschool admissions: No difference

SAT requirement: >700

ACT requirement: mid 30's

Acceptance rate: 7.4%

Acceptance category: Elite/exceptionally competitive

CLEP acceptance policy: No

AP acceptance policy: Credit or advanced standing for a score 4 or better

Transfer credit acceptance policy: None. Dual enrollment not accepted.

Housing: Yes

Co-ed housing: Yes

Athletic programs: Yes

Free undergraduate options: Campus bachelors only, 34 majors

Free distance learning: No

What's free? 100% tuition, room, board, meal plan, study abroad, and books.

What's not? NA

Eligibility: Families earning less than $140,000 per year.

Service requirement: Work-study required, 9 hours per week

Stanford University

450 Serra Mall, Stanford, CA 94305

(650) 723-2300

www.stanford.edu

Type: Private Research University.

Accreditation: Regional

Religious affiliation: No

U.S. News & World Report National Rank: #4 (National) #2 (Engineering) #7 (Undergraduate Teaching)

Regular admissions: Participates in Common Application. SAT, 2 letters of recommendation, personal statement, and transcript

Homeschool admissions: Detailed curriculum description required. Parent's letter may replace teacher's letter. SAT II exam scores encouraged.

SAT requirement: >700

ACT requirement: mid-30's

Acceptance rate: 5.7%

Acceptance category: Elite/exceptionally competitive

CLEP acceptance policy: No

AP acceptance policy: score of 4 or more up to 45 quarter credits

Transfer credit acceptance policy: Transfer credit from regionally accredited colleges considered. Dual enrollment considered for transfer credit.

Housing: Yes

Co-ed housing: Yes

Athletic programs: Yes

Free undergraduate options: Campus bachelors only, 101 majors

Free distance learning: No

What's free? 100% tuition, room, board, meal plan, study abroad, and books.

What's not? NA

Eligibility: Families earning less than $65,000. (Families earning less than $125,000 receive free tuition only)

Service requirement: No

University of Pennsylvania
1 College Hall, Room 100, Philadelphia, PA 19104
(215) 898-5000
www.upenn.edu
Type: Private Research University. Ivy League
Accreditation: Regional
Religious affiliation: No
U.S. News & World Report National Rank: #8 (National) #1 (Undergraduate Business) #26 (Undergraduate Engineering)
Regular admissions: Participates in Common Application. SAT or ACT, 2 SAT II, letters of recommendation, personal statement, and transcript
Homeschool admissions: Detailed curriculum descriptions required. Diploma/GED Not required
SAT requirement: >670
ACT requirement: >31
Acceptance rate: 12%
Acceptance category: Competitive
CLEP acceptance policy: No
AP acceptance policy: Score of 4 or more earns credit
Transfer credit acceptance policy: Dual enrollment courses not accepted if used to meet high school graduation requirements or from 2-year college.
Housing: Yes
Co-ed housing: Yes
Athletic programs: Yes
Free undergraduate options: Campus bachelors only, 90 majors
Free distance learning: No
What's free? 100% tuition, room, board, meal plan, and books.
What's not? Summer classes
Eligibility: Families earning less than $69,999 per year. Families earning less than $130,000 receive 100% tuition
Service requirement: Work study suggested

Yale University
New Haven, CT 06520
(203) 432-4771
www.yale.edu
Type: Private Research University. Ivy League
Accreditation: Regional
Religious affiliation: No
U.S. News & World Report National Rank: #3 (National) #36 (Undergraduate Engineering) #8 (Undergraduate Teaching)
Regular admissions: Participates in Common Application. SAT or ACT, SAT II, letters of recommendation, personal statement, and transcript.
Homeschool admissions: No difference.
SAT requirement: high 700's
ACT requirement: mid 30's
Acceptance rate: 6.3%
Acceptance category: Elite/exceptionally competitive
CLEP acceptance policy: No
AP acceptance policy: Score of 4 or more for credit or placement
Transfer credit acceptance policy: No transfer, online, or dual enrollment courses accepted for incoming freshmen. Limited transfer opportunities for sophomores.
Housing: Yes
Co-ed housing: Yes
Athletic programs: Yes
Free undergraduate options: Campus based bachelors, 75 majors
Free distance learning: No
What's free? 100% tuition, room, board, meal plan, and books.
What's not? NA
Eligibility: Families earning less than $65,000 per year. Families earning up to $100,000 per year receive same package but must pay $4,500 per year.
Service requirement: work study 9-10 hours per week

Jennifer Cook - DeRosa

5 FREE TUITION FOR COLLEGE EMPLOYEES AND THEIR DEPENDENTS

"Every job is good if you do your best and work hard. A man who works hard stinks only to the ones that have nothing to do but smell."
-Laura Ingalls Wilder

Did you know colleges and universities employ hundreds—sometimes thousands—of people to fill a variety of support rolls on campus, and most of them extend tuition benefits to full-time employees and their dependents? Don't make the mistake of assuming that only college professors enjoy benefits like these, because that's completely inaccurate. It's quite possible that a college or university in your town is seeking someone with your skills. In addition to a college's own employment website, my favorite is: www.HigherEdJobs.com.

This option is particularly close to my heart. Why? Because my husband and I left my childhood home to move our family 900 miles across the country so that all four of our children could attend a private university for FREE! My husband is a full-time faculty member at a private university with a hefty price tag. Tuition for four years at this university currently sits around $150,000 for an undergraduate degree. If each of our children graduate from this university, the benefit to our family will exceed $600,000! And it is worth adding that this benefit extends not only to the children, but also to the spouse (me) and employee (my husband). In fact, the university is currently funding 90% towards his MBA degree.

As you consider career and job changes, don't forget to include colleges and universities in your search. The benefits are sometimes immediate and could be worth thousands of dollars. Would I suggest taking a new job to pay for your child's college education? Absolutely! That's what we did.

Jennifer's tip: **When comparing similar job opportunities, choose the school that offers a bachelor's degree. Community colleges offer associate degrees, which typically cost under $10,000 - not a fantastic benefit. On the other hand, a bachelor's degree at a public college will cost at least $50,000 while one from a private university will easily cost $100,000 or more! THAT'S a real deal!**

Non-Academic Jobs and Professions For-Hire on Campus

Alumni Associations/Fundraising
Athletics and Coaching
Broadcasting, Radio, and Television
Bursar and Student Accounts
Business and Financial Services
Child Care
Computer and Information Technology
Conference / Special Events
Counseling / Student Affairs / Advising
Culinary Arts/Kitchen/Food Service
Disability Services
Economic and Business Development
Extension and Outreach
Facilities and Grounds
Health and Medical Services/ Nurses
Human Resources
Instructional Technology and Design
Laboratory and Research
Legal Affairs
Libraries
Museum Staff
Multicultural Affairs and Affirmative Action
Occupational and Environmental Safety
Police and Public Safety
Public Relations, Marketing and Communications
Publications and Editing
Religious Services
Residence Life and Housing
Sales
Secretary and Administrative Assistants / Executive Aid
Sponsored Programs, Grants, and Contracts
Tutors / Adult ESL and Adult Education

Tuition Exchange Members

Tuition Exchange is an amazing consortium of private, public, and religious colleges all over the world! In short, if you can land a job at any college in this section, your child can attend any college in this section. It's like the ultimate reciprocal agreement. In this program, your child doesn't have to attend college where you work, or even stay in your state. Rather, they can attend college at any of the member schools in any state or country.

It's worth noting that there are a few rules which dictate the Tuition Exchange program: First, each school sets its own qualification criteria—while some colleges may allow Tuition Exchange benefits immediately, others may require several years of service. Second, your child will not have an admissions advantage. Your child must meet application deadlines and criteria just like everyone else. Third, some of the schools limit the number of Tuition Exchange participants they'll accept; slots may be limited in some schools. (At the time of printing, there are approximately 6,000 slots open across 630 schools.) Lastly, since each school's tuition rate varies, the amount of the award is capped at $33,000 per year (2015-2016). If your selected institution is more expensive than the award cap, you will have to fund the difference using other means or choose a cheaper school.

For specific information about each member school, visit their own website, or the Tuition Exchange homepage at: www.TuitionExchange.org.

Completely FREE Colleges

ALABAMA

Birmingham-Southern College
900 Arkadelphia Rd, Birmingham, AL 35254

Huntingdon College
1500 E Fairview Ave, Montgomery, AL 36106

Judson College, 302 Bibb St, Marion, AL 36756

Samford University, 800 Lakeshore Drive, Birmingham, AL 35209

Spring Hill College, 4000 Dauphin Street, Mobile, AL 36608

ALASKA

Alaska Pacific University
4101 University Drive, Anchorage, AK 99508

ARIZONA

Arizona Christian University
2625 E Cactus Rd, Phoenix, AZ 85032

Grand Canyon University
3300 W Camelback Rd, Phoenix, AZ 85017

Prescott College, 220 Grove Ave, Prescott, AZ 86301

ARKANSAS

Harding University, 915 E Market Ave, Searcy, AR 72143

Hendrix College, 1600 Washington Ave, Conway, AR 72032

Lyon College, 2300 Highland Rd, Batesville, AR 72503

Ouachita Baptist University
410 Ouachita Street, Arkadelphia, AR 71998

University of the Ozarks, 415 N College Ave, Clarksville, AR 72830

CALIFORNIA

Azusa Pacific University, 901 E Alosta Ave, Azusa, CA 91702

Biola University, 13800 Biola Ave, La Mirada, CA 90639

California Baptist University
8432 Magnolia Ave, Riverside, CA 92504

California Institute of Integral Studies
1453 Mission St, San Francisco, CA 94103

California Lutheran University
60 W Olsen Rd, Thousand Oaks, CA 91360

Chapman University, 1 University Drive Orange, CA 92866

Concordia University, 1530 Concordia West, Irvine, CA 92612

CALIFORNIA

Dominican University of California
50 Acacia Ave, San Rafael, CA 94901

Fresno Pacific University, 1717 S Chestnut Ave, Fresno, CA 93702

Loyola Marymount University
1 Loyola Marymount University Drive, Los Angeles, CA 90045

Marymount California University
30800 Palos Verdes Drive E, Rancho Palos Verdes, CA 90275

Mills College, 5000 MacArthur Blvd, Oakland, CA 94613

Mount Saint Mary's University
12001 Chalon Rd, Los Angeles, CA 90049

Notre Dame De Namur University
1500 Ralston Ave, Belmont, CA 94002

Occidental College, 1600 Campus Rd, Los Angeles, CA 90041

Pepperdine University
24255 Pacific Coast Hwy, Malibu, CA 90263

Saint Mary's College of California
1928 St Mary's Rd, Moraga, CA 94556

Santa Clara University, 500 El Camino Real, Santa Clara, CA 95053

Simpson University, 2211 College View Drive, Redding, CA 96003

Southwestern Law School, 3050 Wilshire Blvd, Los Angeles, CA

CALIFORNIA

University of La Verne, 1950 3rd St, La Verne, CA 91750

University of Redlands, 1200 E Colton Ave, Redlands, CA 92373

University of San Diego, 5998 Alcala Park, San Diego, CA 92110

University of San Francisco
2130 Fulton Street, San Francisco, CA 94117

University of Southern California, Los Angeles, CA 90089

University of the Pacific, 3601 Pacific Ave, Stockton, CA 95211

Vanguard University of Southern California
55 Fair Drive, Costa Mesa, CA 92626

Westmont College, 955 La Paz Rd, Santa Barbara, CA 93108

Whittier College, 13406 Philadelphia St, Whittier, CA 90601

CANADA

King's University College at Western University
266 Epworth Ave, London, ON N6A 2M3, Canada

COLORADO

Johnson & Wales University
7150 Montview Blvd, Denver, Colorado 80220

Regis University, 3333 Regis Boulevard, Denver, Colorado 80221

CONNECTICUT

Connecticut College
270 Mohegan Avenue, New London, CT 06320

Fairfield University, 1073 North Benson Road, Fairfield, CT 06824

Goodwin College, One Riverside Drive, East Hartford, CT 06118

Mitchell College, 437 Pequot Avenue, New London, CT 06320

Quinnipiac University
275 Mount Carmel Avenue, Hamden, Connecticut 06518

Sacred Heart University, 5151 Park Avenue, Fairfield, CT 06825

Trinity College, 300 Summit Street, Hartford CT 06106

University of Bridgeport, 126 Park Avenue, Bridgeport, CT 06604

University of Hartford
200 Bloomfield Avenue, West Hartford, CT 06117

University of New Haven
300 Boston Post Road, West Haven, CT 06516

University of Saint Joseph
1678 Asylum Avenue, West Hartford, Connecticut 06117-2791

DELAWARE

University of Delaware, Newark, DE 19716

Wesley College, 120 North State Street, Dover, Delaware 19901

Wilmington University
320 N. DuPont Hwy, New Castle, DE 19720

DISTRICT OF COLUMBIA

American University
4400 Massachusetts Avenue, NW, Washington, DC 20016

Catholic University of America
620 Michigan Ave., N.E., Washington, DC 20064

George Washington University
2121 Eye Street, NW, Washington, DC 20052

Trinity College of DC
125 Michigan Ave. NE, Washington, DC 20017

FLORIDA

Barry University, 11300 NE 2nd Ave, Miami, FL 33161

Eckerd College, 4200 54th Ave S, St Petersburg, FL 33711

Edward Waters College, 1658 Kings Rd, Jacksonville, FL 32209

FLORIDA

Embry-Riddle Aeronautical University
600 South Clyde Morris Blvd. Daytona Beach, FL 32114

Flagler College, 74 King St, St. Augustine, FL 32084

Florida Institute of Technology
150 W University Blvd, Melbourne, FL 32901

Florida Southern College
111 Lake Hollingsworth Drive, Lakeland, FL 33801

Jacksonville University
2800 University Blvd, Jacksonville, FL 32211

Johnson & Wales University
1701 NE 127th St, North Miami, FL 33181

Lynn University, 3601 N Military Trail, Boca Raton, FL 33431

New College of Florida, 5800 Bay Shore Rd, Sarasota, FL 34243

Palm Beach Atlantic University
901 S Flagler Drive, West Palm Beach, FL 33401

Rollins College, 1000 Holt Ave, Winter Park, FL 32789

Saint Leo University, 33701 State Route 52, St Leo, FL 33574

St. Thomas University
16401 NW 37th Ave, Miami Gardens, FL 33054

Stetson University, 421 N Woodland Blvd, DeLand, FL 32723

FLORIDA

University of Florida, Gainesville, FL 32611

University of North Florida
1 University of North Fl. Drive, Jacksonville, FL 32224

University of Tampa, 401 W Kennedy Blvd, Tampa, FL 33606

GEORGIA

Agnes Scott College, 141 E College Ave, Decatur, GA 30030

Andrew College, 501 College St, Cuthbert, GA 39840

Berry College
2277 Martha Berry Highway NW, Mt Berry, GA 30149

Brenau University, 500 Washington St SE, Gainesville, GA 30501

Covenant College
14049 Scenic Hwy, Lookout Mountain, GA 30750

LaGrange College, 601 Broad St, LaGrange, GA 30240

Mercer University
1501 Mercer University Drive, Macon, GA 31207

Oglethorpe University, 4484 Peachtree Rd, Atlanta, GA 30319

Shorter University, 315 Shorter Ave, Rome, GA 30165

Toccoa Falls College, 107 Kincaid Drive, Toccoa Falls, GA 30598

GEORGIA

Truett-McConnell College
100 Alumni Drive, Cleveland, GA 30528

Wesleyan College, 4760 Forsyth Rd, Macon, GA 31210

GREECE

American College of Greece, Agia Paraskevi, Greece

IDAHO

College of Idaho, 2112 Cleveland Blvd, Caldwell, ID 83605

ILLINOIS

Augustana College, 639 38th St, Rock Island, IL 61201

Aurora University, 347 S Gladstone Ave, Aurora, IL 60506

Benedictine University, 5700 College Rd, Lisle, IL 60532

Blackburn College, 700 College Ave #1, Carlinville, IL 62626

Bradley University, 1501 W Bradley Ave, Peoria, IL 61625

Columbia College Chicago
600 S Michigan Ave, Chicago, IL 60605

ILLINOIS

Concordia University, 7400 Augusta St, River Forest, IL 60305

DePaul University, 2320 N Kenmore Ave, Chicago, IL 60614

Dominican University, 7900 Division St, River Forest, IL 60305

Elmhurst College, 190 S Prospect Ave, Elmhurst, IL 60126

Illinois College, 1101 W College Ave, Jacksonville, IL 62650

Illinois Institute of Technology
3300 S Federal St, Chicago, IL 60616

John Marshall Law School, 315 S Plymouth Ct, Chicago, IL 60604

Judson University, 1151 N State St, Elgin, IL 60123

Knox College, 2 E South St, Galesburg, IL 61401

Lewis University, 1 University Pkwy, Romeoville, IL 60446

MacMurray College, 447 E College Ave, Jacksonville, IL 62650

McKendree University, 701 College Rd, Lebanon, IL 62254

Methodist College, 415 NE St Mark Ct, Peoria, IL 61603

Millikin University, 1184 W Main St, Decatur, IL 62522

Monmouth College, 700 E Broadway, Monmouth, IL 61462

National-Louis University, 122 S Michigan Ave, Chicago, IL 60603

ILLINOIS

North Central College, 30 N Brainard St, Naperville, IL 60540

North Park University, 3225 W Foster Ave, Chicago, IL 60625

Northern Baptist Theological Seminary
660 Butterfield Rd, Lombard, IL 60148

Quincy University, 1800 College Ave, Quincy, IL 62301

Robert Morris University, 401 S State St, Chicago, IL 60605

Rockford University, 5050 E State St, Rockford, IL 61108

Roosevelt University, 430 S Michigan Ave, Chicago, IL 60605

Saint Xavier University, 3700 W 103rd St, Chicago, IL 60655

School of the Art Institute of Chicago
36 S. Wabash Ave #1210, Chicago, IL 60603

Trinity International University
2065 Half Day Rd, Deerfield, IL 60015

University of St. Francis, 500 Wilcox St, Joliet, IL 60435

INDIANA

Anderson University, 1100 E 5th St, Anderson, IN 46012

Butler University, 4600 Sunset Ave, Indianapolis, IN 46208

INDIANA

Calumet College of Saint Joseph
2400 New York Ave, Whiting, IN 46394

DePauw University, Greencastle, IN 46135

Franklin College, 101 Branigin Blvd, Franklin, IN 46131

Hanover College, 484 Ball Dr., Hanover, IN 47243

Holy Cross College, 54515 IN-933, Notre Dame, IN 46556

Huntington University, 2303 College Ave, Huntington, IN 46750

Indiana Institute of Technology
1600 E Washington Blvd, Fort Wayne, IN 46803

Manchester University
604 E College Ave, North Manchester, IN 46962

Marian University, 3200 Cold Spring Rd, Indianapolis, IN 46222

Oakland City University,
138 N Lucretia St, Oakland City, IN 47660

Rose-Hulman Institute of Technology
5500 Wabash Ave, Terre Haute, IN 47803

Saint Joseph's College, 1498 S College Ave, Rensselaer, IN 47978

Saint Mary-of-the-Woods College
1 St Mary of Woods College, St Mary-Of-The-Woods, IN 47876

INDIANA

Trine University, 1 University Ave, Angola, IN 46703

University of Evansville, 1800 Lincoln Ave, Evansville, IN 47714

University of Indianapolis
1400 E Hanna Ave, Indianapolis, IN 46227

University of Saint Francis, 2701 Spring St, Fort Wayne, IN 46808

Valparaiso University, 1700 Chapel Dr., Valparaiso, IN 46383

Wabash College, 301 W Wabash Ave, Crawfordsville, IN 47933

IOWA

AIB College of Business, 2500 Fleur Dr., Des Moines, IA 50321

Briar Cliff University, 3303 Rebecca St, Sioux City, IA 51104

Buena Vista University, 610 W 4th St, Storm Lake, IA 50588

Central College, 812 University St, Pella, IA 50219

Clarke University, 1550 Clarke Dr, Dubuque, IA 52001

Coe College, 1220 1st Ave NE, Cedar Rapids, IA 52402

Cornell College, 600 1st Street Southwest, Mt Vernon, IA 52314

Drake University, 2507 University Ave, Des Moines, IA 50311

IOWA

Graceland University, 1 University Pl, Lamoni, IA 50140

Grand View University
1200 Grandview Ave, Des Moines, IA 50316

Iowa Wesleyan College, 601 N Main St, Mt Pleasant, IA 52641

Loras College, 1450 Alta Vista St, Dubuque, IA 52001

Luther College, 700 College Dr., Decorah, IA 52101

Mercy College of Health Sciences
928 6th Ave, Des Moines, IA 50309

Morningside College, Morningside College - IA

Mount Mercy University
1330 Elmhurst Drive, NE, Cedar Rapids, IA 52402

Simpson College, 701 N C St, Indianola, IA 50125

St. Ambrose University, 518 W Locust St, Davenport, IA 52803

University of Dubuque, 2000 University Ave, Dubuque, IA 52001

Upper Iowa University, 605 Washington St, Fayette, IA 52142

Wartburg College, 100 Keystone Ave, Waverly, IA 50677

William Penn University, Trueblood Ave, Oskaloosa, IA 52577

KANSAS

Baker University, 618 Eighth St, Baldwin City, KS 66006

Benedictine College, 1020 N 2nd St, Atchison, KS 66002

Friends University, 2100 W University St, Wichita, KS 67213

Kansas Wesleyan University, 100 E Claflin Ave, Salina, KS 67401

Newman University, 3100 McCormick St, Wichita, KS 67213

Ottawa University, 1001 S Cedar St, Ottawa, KS 66067

Southwestern College, 100 College St, Winfield, KS 67156

KENTUCKY

Bellarmine University, 2001 Newburg Rd, Louisville, KY 40205

Berea College, 101 Chestnut St, Berea, KY 40403

Brescia University, 717 Frederica St, Owensboro, KY 42301

Centre College, 600 W Walnut St, Danville, KY 40422

Georgetown College, 400 E College St, Georgetown, KY 40324

Kentucky State University, 400 E Main St, Frankfort, KY 40601

Kentucky Wesleyan College
3000 Frederica St, Owensboro, KY 42301

KENTUCKY

Lindsey Wilson College
210 Lindsey Wilson St, Columbia, KY 42728

Midway College, 512 E Stephens St, Midway, KY 40347

Thomas More College
333 Thomas More Pkwy, Crestview Hills, KY 41017

Transylvania University
300 N Broadway, Lexington, KY 40508

Union College, 310 College St, Barbourville, KY 40906

University of the Cumberlands
6178 College Station Dr, Williamsburg, KY 40769

LOUISIANA

Centenary College, 2911 Centenary Blvd, Shreveport, LA 71104

Louisiana Tech University, 305 Wisteria St, Ruston, LA 71272

Tulane University, 6823 St Charles Ave, New Orleans, LA 70118

MAINE

Maine College of Art, 522 Congress St, Portland, ME 04101

Saint Joseph's College of Maine
278 Whites Bridge Rd, Standish, ME 04084

MAINE

University of New England
11 Hills Beach Rd, Biddeford, ME 04005

MARYLAND

Goucher College, 1021 Dulaney Valley Rd, Baltimore, MD 21204

Hood College, 401 Rosemont Ave, Frederick, MD 21701

Loyola University Maryland
4501 N Charles St, Baltimore, MD 21210

Maryland Institute College of Art
1300 W Mt Royal Ave, Baltimore, MD 21217

McDaniel College, 2 College Hill, Westminster, MD 21157

Mount St. Mary's University
16300 Old Emmitsburg Rd, Emmitsburg, MD 21727

Notre Dame of Maryland University
4701 N Charles St, Baltimore, MD 21210

St. Mary's College of Maryland
18952 E Fishers Rd, St Marys City, MD 20686

Stevenson University
1525 1525 Greenspring Valley Road, Stevenson, MD 21153

Washington College
300 Washington Ave, Chestertown, MD 21620

MASSACHUSETTS

Anna Maria College, 50 Sunset Ln, Paxton, MA 01612

Assumption College, 500 Salisbury St, Worcester, MA 01609

Bard College at Simon's Rock
84 Alford Rd, Great Barrington, MA 01230

Bay Path University
588 Longmeadow St, Longmeadow, MA 01106

Becker College, 61 Sever St, Worcester, MA 01609

Boston University, One Silber Way, Boston, MA 02215

Clark University, 950 Main St, Worcester, MA 01610

Curry College, 1071 Blue Hill Avenue, Milton, MA 02186

Dean College, 99 Main St, Franklin, MA 02038

Elms College, 291 Springfield St, Chicopee, MA 01013

Emerson College, 120 Boylston St, Boston, MA 02116

Emmanuel College, 400 Fenway, Boston, MA 02115

Endicott College, 376 Hale St, Beverly, MA 01915

Fisher College, 118 Beacon St, Boston, MA 02116

Hampshire College, 893 West St, Amherst, MA 01002

MASSACHUSETTS

Hellenic College Holy Cross
50 Goddard Ave, Brookline, MA 02445

Lasell College
1844 Commonwealth Avenue, Auburndale, MA 02466

Lesley University, 29 Everett St, Cambridge, MA 02138

Merrimack College, 315 Turnpike St, North Andover, MA 01845

Mount Holyoke College, 50 College St, South Hadley, MA 01075

Mount Ida College, 777 Dedham Street, Newton, MA 02459

National Graduate School of Quality Management
184 Jones Rd # C, Falmouth, MA 02540

Newbury College, 129 Fisher Ave, Brookline, MA 02445

Nichols College, 124 Center Rd, Dudley, MA 01571

Pine Manor College, 400 Heath St, Chestnut Hill, MA 02467

Regis College, 235 Wellesley St, Weston, MA 02493

Simmons College, 300 Fenway, Boston, MA 02115

Smith College, Northampton, MA 01063

Springfield College, 263 Alden St, Springfield, MA 01109

Stonehill College, 320 Washington St, North Easton, MA 02357

MASSACHUSETTS

Suffolk University, 8 Ashburton Pl, Boston, MA 02108

Western New England University
1215 Wilbraham Rd, Springfield, MA 01119

Wheelock College, 200 Riverway, Boston, MA 02215

Worcester Polytechnic Institute
100 Institute Rd, Worcester, MA 01609

MICHIGAN

Adrian College, 110 S Madison St, Adrian, MI 49221

Alma College, 614 W Superior St, Alma, MI 48801

Aquinas College, 1607 Robinson Rd SE, Grand Rapids, MI 49506

Hillsdale College, 33 E College St, Hillsdale, MI 49242

Kettering University, 1700 University Ave, Flint, MI 48504

Lawrence Technological University
21000 W 10 Mile Rd, Southfield, MI 48075

Madonna University, 36600 Schoolcraft Rd, Livonia, MI 48150

Marygrove College, 8425 W McNichols Rd, Detroit, MI 48221

Northwood University, 4000 Whiting Dr, Midland, MI 48640

MICHIGAN

Olivet College, 320 S Main St, Olivet, MI 49076

Walsh College, 3838 Livernois Rd, Troy, MI 48083

Wayne State University, 42 W Warren Ave, Detroit, MI 48202

Western Theological Seminary, 101 E 13th St, Holland, MI 49423

MINNESOTA

Augsburg College, 2211 Riverside Ave, Minneapolis, MN 55454

Bethel University, 3900 Bethel Drive St. Paul, MN 55112

College of St. Scholastica, 1200 Kenwood Ave, Duluth, MN 55811

Concordia College at Moorhead
901 8th St S, Moorhead, MN 56562

Crown College, 8700 College View Dr, St Bonifacius, MN 55375

Gustavus Adolphus College
800 W College Ave, St Peter, MN 56082

Hamline University, 1536 Hewitt Ave, St Paul, MN 55104

Minneapolis College of Art & Design
2501 Stevens Ave, Minneapolis, MN 55404

Saint John's University College of St. Benedict
2850 Abbey Rd, Collegeville, MN 56321

MINNESOTA

Saint Mary's University, 700 Terrace Heights, Winona, MN 55987

St. Catherine University, 2004 Randolph Ave, St Paul, MN 55105

University of Northwestern - St. Paul
3003 Snelling Ave N, St Paul, MN 55113

University of St. Thomas, 2115 Summit Ave, St Paul, MN 55105

William Mitchell College of Law
875 Summit Ave, St Paul, MN 55104

MISSISSIPPI

Belhaven University, 1500 Peachtree St, Jackson, MS 39202

Millsaps College, 1701 N State St, Jackson, MS 39202

Mississippi College, 200 S Capitol St, Clinton, MS 39058

Reformed Theological Seminary
5422 Clinton Blvd., Jackson, MS 39209

MISSOURI

Avila University, 11901 Wornall Rd, Kansas City, MO 64145

Columbia College, 1001 Rogers St, Columbia, MO 65201

Culver-Stockton College, 1 College Hill, Canton, MO 63435

MISSOURI

Drury University, 900 N Benton Ave, Springfield, MO 65802

Fontbonne University, 6800 Wydown Blvd, Clayton, MO 63105

Kansas City Art Institute
4415 Warwick Blvd, Kansas City, MO 64111

Maryville University
650 Maryville University Drive, St. Louis, MO 63141

Missouri Baptist University
One College Park Drive, St. Louis, MO 63141

Northwest Missouri State University
800 University Drive, Maryville, MO 64468

Park University, 8700 NW River Park Drive, Parkville, MO 64152

Rockhurst University, 1100 Rockhurst Rd, Kansas City, MO 64110

Saint Louis University, 1 North Grand, Saint Louis, MO 63103

Southwest Baptist University
1600 University Ave, Bolivar, MO 65613

Stephens College, 1200 E Broadway, Columbia, MO 65215

Webster University
470 E Lockwood Ave, Webster Groves, MO 63119

Westminster College, 501 Westminster Ave, Fulton, MO 65251

MISSOURI

William Jewell College, 500 College Hill, Liberty, MO 64068

William Woods University, 1 University Ave, Fulton, MO 65251

MONTANA

Carroll College, 1601 N Benton Ave, Helena, MT 59625

Rocky Mountain College, 1511 Poly Dr, Billings, MT 59102

University of Great Falls, 1301 20th St S, Great Falls, MT 59405

MOROCCO

Al Akhawayn University in Ifrane
Hassan II Avenue, Ifrane, Meknès-Tafilalet Region, 53000, Morocco

NEBRASKA

College of Saint Mary, 7000 Mercy Rd, Omaha, NE 68106

Concordia University, 800 N Columbia Ave, Seward, NE 68434

Creighton University, 2500 California Plaza, Omaha, NE 68102

Doane College, 1014 Boswell Ave, Crete, NE 68333

Hastings College, 710 Turner Ave, Hastings, NE 68901

NEBRASKA

Nebraska Methodist College, 720 N 87th St, Omaha, NE 68114

Nebraska Wesleyan University
5000 St Paul Ave, Lincoln, NE 68504

NEVADA

Sierra Nevada College, 999 Tahoe Blvd, Incline Village, NV 89451

NEW HAMPSHIRE

Antioch University New England, 40 Avon St, Keene, NH 03431

Colby-Sawyer College, 541 Main St, New London, NH 03257

Franklin Pierce University, 40 University Dr, Rindge, NH 03461

New England College, 98 Bridge St, Henniker, NH 03242

New Hampshire Institute of Art
148 Concord St, Manchester, NH 03104

Saint Anselm College, 100 St Anselm Dr, Manchester, NH 03102

Southern New Hampshire University
2500 N River Rd, Hooksett, NH 03106

NEW JERSEY

Bloomfield College, 467 Franklin St, Bloomfield, NJ 07003

Caldwell University, 120 Bloomfield Ave, Caldwell, NJ 07006

Centenary College, 400 Jefferson St, Hackettstown, NJ 07840

College of Saint Elizabeth, 2 Convent Rd, Morristown, NJ 07960

Drew University, 36 Madison Ave, Madison, NJ 07940

Fairleigh Dickinson University, 1000 River Rd, Teaneck, NJ 07666

Georgian Court University, 900 Lakewood Ave, Lakewood, NJ

Monmouth University
400 Cedar Ave, West Long Branch, NJ 07764

Rider University
2083 Lawrenceville Rd, Lawrence Township, NJ 08648

Saint Peter's University
2641 John F. Kennedy Blvd, Jersey City, NJ 07306

Seton Hall University, 400 S Orange Ave, South Orange, NJ 07079

Stevens Institute of Technology
1 Castle Point Terrace, Hoboken, NJ 07030

Stockton University of NJ
101 Vera King Farris Drive, Galloway, NJ 08205

NEW YORK

Adelphi University, 1 South Ave, Garden City, NY 11530

Albany Law School, 80 New Scotland Ave, Albany, NY 12208

Alfred University, 1 Saxon Drive Alfred, NY 14802

Bard College, 30 Campus Rd, Annandale-On-Hudson, NY 12504

Canisius College, 2001 Main St, Buffalo, NY 14208

Cazenovia College, 22 Sullivan St, Cazenovia, NY 13035

Clarkson University, 8 Clarkson Ave, Potsdam, NY 13699

College of Mount Saint Vincent
6301 Riverdale Ave, Bronx, NY 10471

College of New Rochelle
144 W 125th St #5, New York, NY 10027

College of Saint Rose, 432 Western Ave, Albany, NY 12203

Concordia College, 171 White Plains Rd, Bronxville, NY 10708

Daemen College, 4380 Main St, Amherst, NY 14226

Dominican College of Blauvelt
470 Western Hwy S, Orangeburg, NY 10962

D'Youville College, 320 Porter Ave, Buffalo, NY 14201

Elmira College, 1 Park Pl, Elmira, NY 14901

NEW YORK

Fordham University, 441 E Fordham Rd, Bronx, NY 10458

Hartwick College, 1 Hartwick Dr, Oneonta, NY 13820

Hilbert College, 5200 South Park Ave, Hamburg, NY 14075

Hobart and William Smith Colleges
300 Pulteney St, Geneva, NY 14456

Hofstra University, Hempstead, NY 11549

Houghton College, 1 Willard Ave, Houghton, NY 14744

Iona College, 715 North Ave, New Rochelle, NY 10801

Keuka College, 141 Central Ave, Keuka Park, NY 14478

Le Moyne College, 1419 Salt Springs Rd, Syracuse, NY 13214

Long Island University, Brooklyn Campus
1 University Plaza, Brooklyn, NY 11201

Long Island University, LIU Post
720 Northern Blvd, Brookville, NY 11548

Manhattan College
4513 Manhattan College Pkwy, Bronx, NY 10471

Manhattanville College, 2900 Purchase St, Purchase, NY 10577

Marymount Manhattan College
221 E 71st St, New York, NY 10021

NEW YORK

Medaille College, 18 Agassiz Cir, Buffalo, NY 14214

Mercy College , 555 Broadway, Dobbs Ferry, NY 10522

Molloy College , 1000 Hempstead Ave, Rockville Centre, NY 11570

Mount Saint Mary College, 330 Powell Ave, Newburgh, NY 12550

Nazareth College, 4245 East Ave, Rochester, NY 14618

New York Institute of Technology
1855 Broadway, New York, NY 10023

Niagara University, 5795 Lewiston Rd, Niagara Univ, NY 14109

Nyack College, 2 Washington St, New York, NY 10004

Pace University, 1 Pace Plaza, New York, NY 10038

Paul Smith's College of Arts & Sciences
7777 NY-30, Paul Smiths, NY 12970

Polytechnic Institute of NYU
6 Metro Tech Roadway, Brooklyn, NY 11201

Pratt Institute, 200 Willoughby Ave, Brooklyn, NY 11205

Roberts Wesleyan College
2301 Westside Drive, Rochester, NY 14624

Rochester Institute of Technology
1 Lomb Memorial Drive, Rochester, NY 14623

NEW YORK

Sage College, 140 New Scotland Ave, Albany, NY 12208

Sarah Lawrence College, 1 Mead Way, Yonkers, NY 10708

Skidmore College, 815 N Broadway, Saratoga Springs, NY 12866

St. Bonaventure University
3261 W State Rd, St Bonaventure, NY 14778

St. Francis College, 180 Remsen St, Brooklyn, NY 11201

St. John Fisher College, 3690 East Ave, Rochester, NY 14618

St. John's University, 8000 Utopia Pkwy, Jamaica, NY 11439

St. Joseph's College, 245 Clinton Ave, Brooklyn, NY 11205

St. Lawrence University, 245 Clinton Ave, Brooklyn, NY 11205

St. Thomas Aquinas College, 125 NY-340, Sparkill, NY 10976

Syracuse University, 900 South Crouse Ave, Syracuse, NY 13244

Trocaire College, 360 Choate Ave, Buffalo, NY 14220

Union Graduate College, 80 Nott Terrace, Schenectady, NY 12308

Utica College, 1600 Burrstone Rd, Utica, NY 13502

Vaughn College, 8601 23rd Ave, East Elmhurst, NY 11369

Villa Maria College, 240 Pine Ridge Rd, Buffalo, NY 14225

NEW YORK

Wagner College, 1 Campus Rd, Staten Island, NY 10301

Webb Institute, 298 Crescent Beach Rd, Glen Cove, NY 11542

Wells College, 170 Main St, Aurora, NY 13026

NORTH CAROLINA

Barton College
200 Atlantic Christian Col Dr NE, Wilson, NC 27893

Belmont Abbey College
100 Belmont Mt Holly Rd, Belmont, NC 28012

Campbell University, 143 Main St, Buies Creek, NC 27506

Catawba College, 2300 W Innes St, Salisbury, NC 28144

Chowan University, 1 University Dr, Murfreesboro, NC 27855

Elon University, 100 Campus Drive, Elon, NC 27244

Gardner-Webb University
110 S Main St, Boiling Springs, NC 28017

Greensboro College, 815 W Market St, Greensboro, NC 27401

Guilford College, 5800 W Friendly Ave, Greensboro, NC 27410

High Point University
833 Montlieu Avenue, High Point, NC 27268

NORTH CAROLINA

Johnson & Wales University
801 W Trade St, Charlotte, NC 28202

Lees-McRae College, 191 Main St W, Banner Elk, NC 28604

Lenoir-Rhyne University, 625 7th Ave NE, Hickory, NC 28601

Mars Hill University, 100 Athletic St, Mars Hill, NC 28754

Meredith College, 3800 Hillsborough St, Raleigh, NC 27607

Methodist University, 5400 Ramsey St, Fayetteville, NC 28311

Mid-Atlantic Christian University
715 N Poindexter St, Elizabeth City, NC 27909

North Carolina Wesleyan College
3400 N Wesleyan Blvd, Rocky Mount, NC 27804

Pfeiffer University, 48380 US-52, Misenheimer, NC 28109

Queens University of Charlotte
1900 Selwyn Ave, Charlotte, NC 28207

Salem Academy & College
601 S Church St, Winston-Salem, NC 27101

St. Andrews University
1700 Dogwood Mile St, Laurinburg, NC 28352

Warren Wilson College
7011 Warren Wilson Rd, Swannanoa, NC 28778

NORTH CAROLINA

Wingate University, 220 N Camden Rd, Wingate, NC 28174

OHIO

Ashland University, 401 College Ave, Ashland, OH 44805

Baldwin Wallace University, 275 Eastland Rd, Berea, OH 44017

Bluffton University, 1 University Drive, Bluffton, OH 45817

Capital University, 1 College Ave, Bexley, OH 43209

Case Western Reserve University
10900 Euclid Ave, Cleveland, OH 44106

Cleveland Institute of Art, 11610 Euclid Ave, Cleveland, OH 44106

College of Wooster, 1189 Beall Ave, Wooster, OH 44691

Columbus College of Art & Design
60 Cleveland Ave, Columbus, OH 43215

Defiance College, 701 N Clinton St, Defiance, OH 43512

Franklin University, 201 S Grant Ave, Columbus, OH 43215

Heidelberg University, 310 E Market St, Tiffin, OH 44883

Hiram College, 6832 Hinsdale St, Hiram, OH 44234

OHIO

John Carroll University
1 John Carroll Blvd, University Heights, OH 44118

Lake Erie College, 391 W Washington St, Painesville, OH 44077

Lourdes University, 6832 Convent Blvd, Sylvania, OH 43560

Malone University, 2600 Cleveland Ave NW, Canton, OH 44709

Marietta College, 215 5th St, Marietta, OH 45750

Mercy College of Northwest Ohio
2221 Madison Ave, Toledo, OH 43604

Mount St. Joseph University
5701 Delhi Rd, Cincinnati, OH 45233

Mount Vernon Nazarene University
800 Martinsburg Rd, Mt Vernon, OH 43050

Muskingum University
163 Stormont St, New Concord, OH 43762

Notre Dame College, 4545 College Rd, South Euclid, OH 44121

Ohio Dominican University
1216 Sunbury Road, Columbus, OH 43219

Ohio Northern University, 525 S Main St, Ada, OH 45810

Ohio Wesleyan University, 61 S Sandusky St, Delaware, OH 43015

OHIO

Otterbein University, 1 S Grove St, Westerville, OH 43081

Tiffin University, 155 Miami St, Tiffin, OH 44883

University of Dayton, 300 College Park, Dayton, OH 45469

University of Findlay, 1000 N Main St, Findlay, OH 45840

University of Mount Union, 1972 Clark Ave, Alliance, OH 44601

Ursuline College, 2550 Lander Rd, Pepper Pike, OH 44124

Walsh University, 2020 E Maple St, North Canton, OH 44720

Wilmington College, 1870 Quaker Way, Wilmington, OH 45177

Wittenberg University, 200 W Ward St, Springfield, OH 45504

Xavier University, 3800 Victory Pkwy, Cincinnati, OH 45207

OKLAHOMA

Oklahoma City University
2501 N Blackwelder Ave, Oklahoma City, OK 73106

University of Tulsa, 800 S Tucker Dr, Tulsa, OK 74104

OREGON

Concordia University – Portland
2811 NE Holman St, Portland, OR 97211

George Fox University, 414 N Meridian St, Newberg, OR 97132

Lewis & Clark College
0615 SW Palatine Hill Rd, Portland, OR 97219

Linfield College, 900 SE Baker St, McMinnville, OR 97128

Marylhurst University, 17600 Pacific Hwy, Marylhurst, OR 97036

Pacific University, 2043 College Way, Forest Grove, OR 97116

University of Portland
5000 N Willamette Blvd, Portland, OR 97203

Warner Pacific College, 2219 SE 68th Ave, Portland, OR 97215

Willamette University, 900 State St, Salem, OR 97301

PENNSYLVANIA

Albright College, 1621 N 13th St, Reading, PA 19604

Allegheny College, 520 N Main St, Meadville, PA 16335

Alvernia University, 400 St Bernardine St, Reading, PA 19607

Arcadia University, 450 S Easton Rd, Glenside, PA 19038

PENNSYLVANIA

Bucknell University, 701 Moore Ave, Lewisburg, PA 17837

Cabrini College, 610 King of Prussia Rd, Radnor, PA 19087

Carlow University, 3333 Fifth Ave, Pittsburgh, PA 15213

Cedar Crest College, 100 College Drive, Allentown, PA 18104

Chatham University, 1 Woodland Rd, Pittsburgh, PA 15232

Chestnut Hill College
9601 Germantown Ave, Philadelphia, PA 19118

Delaware Valley University
700 E Butler Ave, Doylestown, PA 18901

DeSales University, 2755 Station Ave, Center Valley, PA 18034

Dickinson College, 28 N College St, Carlisle, PA 17013

Drexel University, 3141 Chestnut St, Philadelphia, PA 19104

Duquesne University, 600 Forbes Ave, Pittsburgh, PA 15282

Eastern University, 1300 Eagle Rd, St Davids, PA 19087

Elizabethtown College, 1 Alpha Drive, Elizabethtown, PA 17022

Franklin & Marshall College
415 Harrisburg Ave, Lancaster, PA 17603

Gannon University, 109 University Square, Erie, PA 16501

PENNSYLVANIA

Geneva College, 3200 College Ave, Beaver Falls, PA 15010

Gettysburg College, 300 N Washington St, Gettysburg, PA 17325

Grove City College, 100 Campus Drive, Grove City, PA 16127

Gwynedd Mercy University
1325 Sumneytown Pike, Gwynedd Valley, PA 19437

Holy Family University
9801 Frankford Ave, Philadelphia, PA 19114

Immaculata University, 1145 King Rd, Immaculata, PA 19345

Juniata College, 1700 Moore St, Huntingdon, PA 16652

Keystone College, 1 College Rd, La Plume, PA 18440

King's College, 133 N River St, Wilkes-Barre, PA 18702

La Roche College, 9000 Babcock Blvd, Pittsburgh, PA 15237

Lafayette College, 730 High St, Easton, PA 18042

LaSalle University, 1900 W Olney Ave, Philadelphia, PA 19141

Lebanon Valley College, 101 College Ave, Annville, PA 17003

Lycoming College, 700 College Pl, Williamsport, PA 17701

Marywood University, 2300 Adams Ave, Scranton, PA 18509

PENNSYLVANIA

Mercyhurst University, 501 E 38th St, Erie, PA 16546

Misericordia University, 301 Lake Street, Dallas, PA 18612

Moore College of Art and Design
1916 Race St, Philadelphia, PA 19103

Moravian College, 1200 Main St, Bethlehem, PA 18018

Mount Aloysius College
7373 Admiral Peary Hwy, Cresson, PA 16630

Muhlenberg College, 2400 W Chew St, Allentown, PA 18104

Neumann University, 1 Neumann Drive, Aston, PA 19014

Peirce College, 1420 Pine St, Philadelphia, PA 19102

Philadelphia University, 4201 Henry Ave, Philadelphia, PA 19144

Pittsburgh Theological Seminary
616 N Highland Ave, Pittsburgh, PA 15206

Point Park University, 201 Wood St, Pittsburgh, PA 15222

Princeton Theological Seminary
64 Mercer St, Princeton, NJ 08540

Robert Morris University, 6001 University Blvd, Moon, PA 15108

Rosemont College, 1400 Montgomery Ave, Bryn Mawr, PA 19010

PENNSYLVANIA

Saint Francis University, 117 Evergreen Drive, Loretto, PA 15940

Saint Joseph's University, 5600 City Ave, Philadelphia, PA 19131

Saint Vincent College, 300 Fraser Purchase Rd, Latrobe, PA 15650

Seton Hill University, 1 Seton Hill Drive, Greensburg, PA 15601

Susquehanna University
514 University Ave, Selinsgrove, PA 17870

The Commonwealth Medical College
525 Pine St, Scranton, PA 18509

Thiel College, 75 College Ave, Greenville, PA 16125

University of Pittsburgh, 4200 Fifth Ave, Pittsburgh, PA 15260

University of Sciences in Philadelphia
600 S 43rd St, Philadelphia, PA 19104

University of Scranton, 800 Linden St, Scranton, PA 18510

University of the Arts, 320 S Broad St, Philadelphia, PA 19102

Ursinus College, 601 E Main St, Collegeville, PA 19426

Villanova University, 800 Lancaster Ave, Villanova, PA 19085

Washington & Jefferson College
60 S Lincoln St, Washington, PA 15301

PENNSYLVANIA

Waynesburg University, 51 W College St, Waynesburg, PA 15370

Westminster College, 319 S Market St, New Wilmington, PA 16142

Widener University, 1 University Pl, Chester, PA 19013

Wilkes University, 84 W South St, Wilkes-Barre, PA 18701

Wilson College, 1015 Philadelphia Ave, Chambersburg, PA 17201

York College of PA, 441 Country Club Rd, York, PA 17403

RHODE ISLAND

Bryant University
1150 Douglas Turnpike, Smithfield, RI 02917

Johnson & Wales University
8 Abbott Park Pl, Providence, RI 02903

Providence College
1 Cunningham Square, Providence, RI 02918

Roger Williams University
1 Old Ferry Rd, Bristol, RI 02809

Salve Regina University
100 Ochre Point Ave, Newport, RI 02840

SOUTH CAROLINA

Anderson University, 316 Boulevard, Anderson, SC 29621

Charleston Southern University
9200 University Blvd, North Charleston, SC 29406

Coker College, 300 E College Ave, Hartsville, SC 29550

Columbia College
1301 Columbia College Drive, Columbia, SC 29203

Converse College, 580 E Main St, Spartanburg, SC 29302

Erskine College, 2 Washington St, Due West, SC 29639

Furman University, 3300 Poinsett Hwy, Greenville, SC 29613

Limestone College, 1115 College Drive, Gaffney, SC 29340

Newberry College, 2100 College St, Newberry, SC 29108

North Greenville University
7801 N Tigerville Rd, Tigerville, SC 29688

Presbyterian College, 503 S Broad St, Clinton, SC 29325

Southern Wesleyan University
907 Wesleyan Drive, Central, SC 29630

Wofford College, 429 N Church St, Spartanburg, SC 29303

SOUTH DAKOTA

Mount Marty College, 1105 W 8th St, Yankton, SD 57078

University of Sioux Falls, 1101 W 22nd St, Sioux Falls, SD 57105

TENNESSEE

Belmont University, 1900 Belmont Blvd, Nashville, TN 37212

Bryan College, 721 Bryan Drive, Dayton, TN 37321

Carson-Newman College
1646 Russell Ave, Jefferson City, TN 37760

Christian Brothers University, 650 E Pkwy S, Memphis, TN 38104

Emmanuel Christian Seminary
1 Walker Drive, Johnson City, TN 37601

Johnson University, 7900 Johnson Drive, Knoxville, TN 37998

Lee University, 1120 N Ocoee St, Cleveland, TN 37311

Lincoln Memorial University
6965 Cumberland Gap Pkwy, Harrogate, TN 37752

Martin Methodist College, 433 W Madison St, Pulaski, TN 38478

Maryville College
502 E Lamar Alexander Pkwy, Maryville, TN 37804

TENNESSEE

Memphis College of Art, 1930 Poplar Ave, Memphis, TN 38104

Milligan College, 1 Blowers Boulevard, Milligan College, TN 37682

Tennessee Wesleyan College, 204 E College St, Athens, TN 37303

Union University, 1050 Union University Drive, Jackson, TN 38305

University of the South, 735 University Ave, Sewanee, TN 37383

TEXAS

Abilene Christian University, 1600 Campus Ct, Abilene, TX 79601

Austin College, 900 N Grand Ave, Sherman, TX 75090

Baylor University, 1311 S 5th St, Waco, TX 76706

Concordia University at Austin
11400 Concordia University Drive, Austin, TX 78726

Criswell College, 4010 Gaston Ave, Dallas, TX 75246

Dallas Baptist University
3000 Mountain Creek Pkwy, Dallas, TX 75211

East Texas Baptist University
1 One Tiger Drive, Marshall, TX 75670

Hardin-Simmons University, 2200 Hickory St, Abilene, TX 79601

TEXAS

Houston Baptist University
7502 Fondren Rd, Houston, TX 77074

Howard Payne University
1000 Fisk Street, Brownwood, TX 76801

McMurry University, 1400 Sayles Blvd, Abilene, TX 79605

Schreiner University, 2100 San Antonio Hwy, Kerrville, TX 78028

Southwestern University
1001 E University Ave, Georgetown, TX 78626

St. Edward's University, 3001 S Congress Ave, Austin, TX 78704

St. Mary's University
1 Camino Santa Maria, San Antonio, TX 78228

Texas Christian University
2800 S University Drive, Fort Worth, TX 76129

Texas Lutheran University
2800 S University Drive, Fort Worth, TX 76129

Texas Wesleyan University
1201 Wesleyan St, Fort Worth, TX 76105

Trinity University, 1 Trinity Place, San Antonio, TX 78212

University of Dallas, 1845 E Northgate Drive, Irving, TX 75062

TEXAS

University of Mary Hardin-Baylor
900 College St, Belton, TX 76513

University of St. Thomas
2115 Summit Ave, St Paul, MN 55105

University of the Incarnate Word
4301 Broadway St, San Antonio, TX 78209

Wayland Baptist University, 1900 W 7th St, Plainview, TX 79072

UNITED ARAB EMIRATES

American University Sharjah, Sharjah - United Arab Emirates

UTAH

Westminster College, 1840 1300 E, Salt Lake City, UT 84105

VERMONT

Bennington College, 1 College Drive, Bennington, VT 05201

Champlain College, 163 S Willard St, Burlington, VT 05402

College of St. Joseph, Rutland, VT 05701

Goddard College, 123 Pitkin Rd, Plainfield, VT 05667

VERMONT

Green Mountain College, 1 Brennan Cir, Poultney, VT 05764

Landmark College, 19 River Rd S, Putney, VT 05346

Marlboro College, 2582 South Road, Marlboro, VT 05344

Norwich University, 158 Harmon Drive, Northfield, VT 05663

Saint Michael's College
One Winooski Park, Colchester, VT 05439

VIRGIN ISLANDS

University of the Virgin Islands
Charlotte Amalie West, St Thomas, U.S. Virgin Islands

VIRGINIA

Appalachian School of Law
1169 Edgewater Drive, Grundy, VA 24614

Bluefield College, 3000 College Drive, Bluefield, VA 24605

Bridgewater College, 402 E College St, Bridgewater, VA 22812

Emory & Henry College, 30461 Garnand Dr, Emory, VA 24327

Ferrum College
9000 United States, 215 State Rte 602, Ferrum, VA 24088

VIRGINIA

Hampden-Sydney College, 1 College Rd, Farmville, VA 23901

Hollins University, 7916 Williamson Rd, Roanoke, VA 24019

Jefferson College of Health Sciences
101 Elm Avenue Southeast, Roanoke, VA 24013

Lynchburg College, 1501 Lakeside Drive, Lynchburg, VA 24501

Mary Baldwin College, 318 Prospect St, Staunton, VA 24401

Marymount University, 2807 N Glebe Rd, Arlington, VA 22207

Randolph College, 2500 Rivermont Ave, Lynchburg, VA 24503

Randolph-Macon College, 204 Henry St, Ashland, VA 23005

Regent University
1000 Regent University Drive, Virginia Beach, VA 23464

Roanoke College, 221 College Alley, Salem, VA 24153

Shenandoah University
1460 University Drive, Winchester, VA 22601

University of Richmond,
28 Westhampton Way, Richmond, VA 23173

Virginia Wesleyan College
1584 Wesleyan Drive, Norfolk, VA 23502

WASHINGTON

Cornish College of the Arts, 1000 Lenora St, Seattle, WA 98121

Gonzaga University, 502 E Boone Ave, Spokane, WA 99202

Heritage University, 3240 Fort Rd, Toppenish, WA 98948

Pacific Lutheran University
12180 Park Ave S, Tacoma, WA 98447

Saint Martin's University, 5000 Abbey Way SE, Lacey, WA 98503

Seattle University, 901 12th Ave, Seattle, WA 98122

University of Puget Sound, 1500 N Warner St, Tacoma, WA 98416

Whitworth University, 300 W Hawthorne Rd, Spokane, WA 99251

WEST VIRGINIA

Bethany College, 31 E Campus Drive, Bethany, WV 26032

Davis and Elkins College, 100 Campus Drive, Elkins, WV 26241

University of Charleston
2300 Maccorkle Ave SE, Charleston, WV 25304

West Virginia Wesleyan College
59 College Ave, Buckhannon, WV 26201

Wheeling Jesuit University
316 Washington Ave, Wheeling, WV 26003

WISCONSIN

Alverno College
3400 S 43rd St, Milwaukee, WI 53234 Beloit College,

Carroll University, 100 N East Ave, Waukesha, WI 53186

Carthage College, 2001 Alford Park Drive, Kenosha, WI 53140

Columbia College of Nursing
4425 North Port Washington Road, Milwaukee, WI 53212

Concordia University Wisconsin
12800 N Lake Shore Drive, Mequon, WI 53097

Lakeland College, w3718 South Drive, Plymouth, WI 53073

Lawrence University, 711 E Boldt Way, Appleton, WI 54911

Marian University
45 South National Avenue, Fond du Lac, WI 54935

Northland College, 1411 Ellis Ave S, Ashland, WI 54806

Ripon College, 300 Seward St, Ripon, WI 54971

St. Norbert College, 100 Grant St, De Pere, WI 54115

Viterbo University, 900 Viterbo Drive, La Crosse, WI 54601

6 FREE TUITION DURING HIGH SCHOOL

"The tiniest little thing can change the course of your day,
which can change the course of your year, which can change who you are."
-Taylor Swift

It's possible to earn college credit while you're in high school, and it's frequently possible to complete an entire certificate, diploma or degree. The best part, is that you can do this without paying tuition! Students using this strategy participate in dual enrollment programs. In a dual enrollment program, they're earning credit twice, but only taking a class once. The course "double-dips" by meeting the student's high school graduation requirement, and also counting toward their college degree. It's a fantastic opportunity, if you're aware it exists.

Dual enrollment programs are called many things: Career and College Promise, Early College, Postsecondary Enrollment Option, Concurrent Enrollment, Dual Credit, Joint High School, Articulated High School, or others. Dual enrollment programs are available in all 50 states through either public or private colleges. A typical dual enrollment program is open to 11th and 12th grade students, meets high school diploma and college degree requirements simultaneously, offers an assortment of classes, and is open to anyone with the ambition to succeed.

Most states leave it up to individual local school districts to decide the scope of tuition benefits, which means a lot of confusion for parents. This short list identifies whole-state programs. In other words, these states offer free dual enrollment to all students. If your state isn't included, you are among the 13,000 high school districts in the country that determine for themselves if they'll fund a program. Always contact your local community college and your state's department of education. Programs come and go every year.

If you know of a free dual enrollment program in your town, I'd love to hear about it! Drop me a note at CompletelyFREEColleges@aol.com.

COLORADO

Called: Concurrent Enrollment
Contact: Colorado Department of Education
What's free? Community college tuition, unlimited
What's not? Books
Eligibility: 9th grade or higher, not yet 21
Homeschool: Not eligible
Distance learning: undefined

FLORIDA

Called: Dual Enrollment
Contact: Florida Department of Education
What's free? Community college tuition, unlimited
What's not? Books
Eligibility: 6th grade through 12th grade
Homeschool: Yes
Distance learning: Yes

ILLINOIS

Called: Dual Credit
Contact: Your local high school
What's free? Community college tuition
What's not? Books
Eligibility: 9th grade through 12th grade in a specific school district.
Homeschool: Varies
Distance learning: undefined
Other: The state does not fund Dual Credit, however more than 75% of the schools in Illinois do; so I decided to include them.

IOWA

Called: Postsecondary Enrollment Options (PSEO)
Contact: Iowa Department of Education
What's free? Community college tuition and books.
What's not? Supplies that become the property of the student.
Eligibility: all 11th and 12th grade, gifted 9th and 10th grade
Homeschool: Yes
Distance learning: Yes

LOUISIANA

Called: Dual Enrollment
Contact: Louisiana Department of Education; Louisiana Believes
What's free? Technical, community, or 4-year college tuition
What's not? Books
Eligibility: 11th and 12th public school student
Homeschool: Eligible to enroll, but not free.
Distance learning: Yes
Other: 24 college credits=student is eligible for high school diploma.

MICHIGAN

Called: Postsecondary Enrollment Option (PSEO) and Career and Technical Preparation (CTP)
Contact: www.Michigan.gov
What's free? Technical or community college tuition and books.
What's not? Parking and activity fees
Eligibility: Higher than 8th grade with qualifying assessment exam.
Homeschool: Yes, but must enroll in at least 1 public school course.
Distance learning: Yes

NEW MEXICO

Called: Dual Credit
Contact: New Mexico Public Education Department
What's free? Technical or community college tuition
What's not? Lab fees
Eligibility: High school students
Homeschool: Eligible to enroll, but not free
Distance learning: Yes

NORTH CAROLINA

Called: Career and College Promise
Contact: Your local community college
What's free? Community college tuition, unlimited
What's not? Books
Eligibility: 11th and 12th graders (9th and 10th grade in limited instances)
Homeschool: Yes
Distance learning: Yes

OHIO

Called: College Credit Plus
Contact: Ohio Department of Higher Education
What's free? Tuition and books
What's not? NA
Eligibility: 7th grade or higher
Homeschool: Yes
Distance learning: Yes

OREGON

Called: Dual Credit
Contact: Oregon Department of Education
What's free? Tuition
What's not? Book fee dependent on specific program
Eligibility: 9th through 12th grades
Homeschool: Yes
Distance learning: Yes

VERMONT

Called: Dual Enrollment
Contact: Vermont Department of Education
What's free? 2 community college courses per semester.
What's not? Books and fees
Eligibility: 11th and 12th grades
Homeschool: Yes
Distance learning: Yes

VIRGINIA

Called: Dual Enrollment
Contact: Virginia Department of Education
What's free? Community college tuition
What's not? Books
Eligibility: 11th and 12th grades
Homeschool: Yes
Distance learning: Yes

WISCONSIN

Called: Youth Options Program
Contact: Wisconsin Department of Public Instruction
What's free? Community college tuition, books, and fees.
What's not? NA
Eligibility: 11th and 12th grades
Homeschool: Yes
Distance learning: Yes

WYOMING

Called: Dual Enrollment
Contact: Wyoming Department of Education
What's free? Community college tuition, books, and fees.
What's not? NA
Eligibility: 11th and 12th grades
Homeschool: Yes
Distance learning: Yes

7 FREE TUITION FOR SENIOR CITIZENS

"Retirement at sixty-five is ridiculous.
When I was sixty-five I still had pimples."
-George Burns

You're never too old to go back to college, and in many states, it's completely tuition-free! Across the United States, colleges and universities are opening their seats to senior citizens free of charge. The trick is finding these programs and deciding what type of student you'd like to be.

Unlike the traditionally-aged student, senior citizens have the option of taking courses for credit, or on audit. Auditing is the non-credit option that allows full participation, but without the burden of taking exams or earning grades. Since senior citizens don't need the "piece of paper" to launch them into the workforce, so their options are more plentiful than those of a degree-seeking student. In both cases, seniors can have full campus access to enormous libraries, stimulating lectures, musical performances, cultural activities, and all the amenities of a large university.

For the senior who would like to earn a degree, there are a number of states that provide fully-funded degree programs for seniors. If earning a degree is your goal, you'll want to be sure the college understands you'd like to enroll as a degree-seeking student, not as an auditing student.

Auditing / Non-Degree Seeking

No philanthropic organization has created more senior citizen educational opportunities than the Bernard Osher Foundation's Osher Lifelong Learning Institute (OLLI). Over the last 15 years, The Osher Foundation has donated money to fund OLLI programs at more than 118 colleges and universities across the country. Most of the OLLI programs are open to any adult age 50 or more who would like to audit a course, or participate in non-credit learning. OLLI programs emphasize the joy of learning, while offering intellectual stimulation to adult learners. If you don't need a degree, you'll probably find everything you need in an OLLI program. Contact each college directly. The locations of OLLI classes may differ from the primary college address.

ALABAMA

OLLI at Auburn University, Auburn, AL 36849

OLLI at University of Alabama- Huntsville
301 Sparkman Drive NW, Huntsville, AL 35899

OLLI at University of Alabama-Tuscaloosa
Tuscaloosa, AL 35487

ALASKA

OLLI at University of Alaska-Fairbanks
505 S Chandlar Drive, Fairbanks, AK 99775

ARIZONA

OLLI at Arizona State University
1130 E University Drive, Tempe, AZ 85281

OLLI at University of Arizona, Tucson, AZ 85721

OLLI at Yavapai College, 1100 E Sheldon St, Prescott, AZ 86301

ARKANSAS

OLLI at University of Arkansas, Fayetteville, AR 72701

CALIFORNIA

OLLI at California State Monterey Bay
100 Campus Center, Seaside, CA 93955

OLLI at California State University- Channel Islands
1 University Drive, Camarillo, CA 93012

OLLI at California State University- Chico
400 W 1st St, Chico, CA 95929

OLLI at California State University- Dominguez Hills
1000 E Victoria St, Carson, CA 90747

OLLI at California State University- East Bay
25800 Carlos Bee Blvd, Hayward, CA 94542

OLLI at California State University- Fresno
5241 N Maple Ave, Fresno, CA 93740

CALIFORNIA

OLLI at California State University- Fullerton
800 N State College Blvd, Fullerton, CA 92831

OLLI at California State University- Long Beach
1250 Bellflower Blvd, Long Beach, CA 90840

OLLI at California State University- San Bernardino
5500 University Pkwy, San Bernardino, CA 92407

OLLI at California State University- San Marcos
333 S Twin Oaks Valley Rd, San Marcos, CA 92078

OLLI at Dominican University of California
50 Acacia Ave, San Rafael, CA 94901

OLLI at Humboldt State University
1 Harpst St, Arcata, CA 95521

OLLI at San Diego State University
5500 Campanile Drive, San Diego, CA 92182

OLLI at San Francisco State University
1600 Holloway Ave, San Francisco, CA 94132

OLLI at Santa Clara University
500 El Camino Real, Santa Clara, CA 95053

OLLI at Sierra College, 5000 Rocklin Rd, Rocklin, CA 95677

OLLI at Sonoma State University
1801 E Cotati Ave, Rohnert Park, CA 94928

CALIFORNIA

OLLI at University of California-Berkeley, Berkeley, CA

OLLI at University of California-Davis
1 Shields Ave, Davis, CA 95616

OLLI at University of California-Irvine, Irvine, CA 92697

OLLI at University of California-Los Angeles
Los Angeles, CA 90095

OLLI at University of California-Riverside
900 University Ave, Riverside, CA 92521

OLLI at University of California-San Diego
9500 Gilman Dr, La Jolla, CA 92093

OLLI at University of California-Santa Cruz
1156 High St, Santa Cruz, CA 95064

OLLI at University of the Pacific
3601 Pacific Ave, Stockton, CA 95211

COLORADO

OLLI at Colorado State University, Fort Collins, CO 80523

OLLI at University of Denver
2199 S University Blvd, Denver, CO 80208

CONNECTICUT

OLLI at University of Connecticut, Storrs, CT 06269

DELAWARE

OLLI at University of Delaware, Newark, DE 19716

FLORIDA

OLLI at Eckerd College, 4200 54th Ave S, St Petersburg, FL 33711

OLLI at Florida International University
11200 SW 8th St, Miami, FL 33199

OLLI at Florida State University
600 W College Ave, Tallahassee, FL 32306

OLLI at University of Miami
1320 S Dixie Hwy, Coral Gables, FL 33124

OLLI at University of North Florida
1 University of North Florida Drive, Jacksonville, FL 32224

OLLI at University of South Florida
4202 E Fowler Ave, Tampa, FL 33620

GEORGIA

OLLI at Emory University
201 Dowman Drive, Atlanta, GA 30322

OLLI at Kennesaw State University
1000 Chastain Rd, Kennesaw, GA 30144

OLLI at University of Georgia-Athens, Athens, GA 30602

HAWAII

OLLI at University of Hawaii-Manoa
2500 Campus Rd, Honolulu, HI 96822

IDAHO

OLLI at Boise State University
1910 University Drive, Boise, ID 83725

ILLINOIS

OLLI at Northwestern University Professional Studies
405 Church Street, 60208, 405 Church St, Evanston, IL

OLLI at Bradley University, 1501 W Bradley Ave, Peoria, IL 61625

OLLI at University of Illinois, Champaign, IL

INDIANA

OLLI at Indiana State University
200 N 7th St, Terre Haute, IN 47809

IOWA

OLLI at Iowa State University, Ames, IA 50011

KANSAS

OLLI at University of Kansas
1450 Jayhawk Blvd, Lawrence, KS 66045

KENTUCKY

OLLI at University of Kentucky, Lexington, KY 40506

LOUISIANA

OLLI at Louisiana State University, Baton Rouge, LA 70803

MAINE

OLLI at University of Southern Maine
96 Falmouth St, Portland, ME 04103

MARYLAND

OLLI at Johns Hopkins University, Baltimore, MD 21218

OLLI at Towson University, 8000 York Rd, Towson, MD 21252

MASSACHUSETTS

OLLI at Berkshire Community College
1350 West St, Pittsfield, MA 01201

OLLI at Brandeis University , 415 South St, Waltham, MA 02453

OLLI at Tufts University, 419 Boston Ave, Medford, MA 02155

OLLI at University of Massachusetts-Boston
100 Morrissey Boulevard, Boston, MA 02125

MICHIGAN

OLLI at Aquinas College
1607 Robinson Rd SE, Grand Rapids, MI 49506

OLLI at Saginaw Valley State University
7400 Bay Rd, University Center, MI 48710

MICHIGAN

OLLI at University of Michigan
500 S State St, Ann Arbor, MI 48109

OLLI at Western Michigan University
1903 W Michigan Ave, Kalamazoo, MI 49008

MINNESOTA

OLLI at University of Minnesota, Minneapolis, MN 55455

MISSISSIPPI

OLLI at University of Southern Mississippi
118 College Drive, Hattiesburg, MS 39406

MISSOURI

OLLI at University of Missouri-Columbia, Columbia, MO 65211

MONTANA

OLLI at University of Montana-Missoula
32 Campus Drive, Missoula, MT 59812

NEBRASKA

OLLI at University of Nebraska, 1400 R St, Lincoln, NE 68588

NEVADA

OLLI at University of Nevada-Las Vegas
4505 S Maryland Pkwy, Las Vegas, NV 89154

OLLI at University of Nevada-Reno
1664 N Virginia St, Reno, NV 89503

NEW HAMPSHIRE

OLLI at Dartmouth College, Hanover, NH 03755

OLLI at Granite State College
35-E Industrial Way Suite 101 Rochester, NH 03867

NEW JERSEY

OLLI at Rutgers University
176 Ryders Lane, New Brunswick NJ 08901

NEW MEXICO

OLLI at University of New Mexico, Albuquerque, NM 87131

NEW YORK

OLLI at Rochester Institute of Technology
1 Lomb Memorial Drive, Rochester, NY 14623

OLLI at Stony Brook University, Stony Brook, NY 11794

NORTH CAROLINA

OLLI at Duke University, Durham, NC 27708

OLLI at North Carolina State University, Raleigh, NC 27695

OLLI at University of North Carolina-Wilmington
601 S College Rd, Wilmington, NC 28403

OLLI at University of North Carolina-Asheville
1 University Heights, Asheville, NC 28804

NORTH DAKOTA

OLLI at University of North Dakota, Grand Forks, ND

OHIO

OLLI at University of Cincinnati
2600 Clifton Ave, Cincinnati, OH 45220

OLLI at University of Dayton
300 College Park, Dayton, OH 45469

OKLAHOMA

OLLI at Oklahoma State University, Stillwater, OK 74074

OLLI at University of Oklahoma
660 Parrington Oval, Norman, OK 73019

OREGON

OLLI at Southern Oregon University
1250 Siskiyou Blvd, Ashland, OR 97520

OLLI at University of Oregon
1585 E 13th Ave, Eugene, OR 97403

PENNSYLVANIA

OLLI at Carnegie Mellon University
5000 Forbes Ave, Pittsburgh, PA 15213

OLLI at Pennsylvania State University
University Park, State College, PA 16801

OLLI at Temple University
1801 N Broad St, Philadelphia, PA 19122

OLLI at University of Pittsburgh
4200 Fifth Ave, Pittsburgh, PA 15260

OLLI at Widener University, 1 University Pl, Chester, PA 19013

RHODE ISLAND

OLLI at University of Rhode Island
45 Upper College Rd, Kingston, RI 02881

SOUTH CAROLINA

OLLI at Clemson University
101 Calhoun Drive, Clemson, SC 29634

OLLI at Coastal Carolina University
100 Chanticleer Drive E, Conway, SC 29528

OLLI at Furman University
3300 Poinsett Hwy, Greenville, SC 29613

OLLI at University of South Carolina-Beaufort
801 Carteret St, Beaufort, SC 29902

SOUTH DAKOTA

OLLI at University of South Dakota
414 E Clark St, Vermillion, SD 57069

TENNESSEE

OLLI at Vanderbilt University
2201 West End Ave, Nashville, TN 37235

TEXAS

OLLI at Texas Tech University
2500 Broadway, Lubbock, TX 79409

OLLI at University of Texas-Austin, Austin, TX 78712

OLLI at University of Texas-El Paso
500 W University Ave, El Paso, TX 79968

OLLI at University of Texas-Medical Branch
301 University Boulevard, Galveston, TX 77555

UTAH

OLLI at University of Utah
201 Presidents Cir, Salt Lake City, UT 84112

VERMONT

OLLI at University of Vermont, Burlington, VT 05405

VIRGINIA

OLLI at University of Richmond
28 Westhampton Way, Richmond, VA 23173

OLLI at University of Virginia, Charlottesville, VA

WASHINGTON

OLLI at University of Washington, Seattle, WA

WEST VIRGINIA

OLLI at West Virginia University, Morgantown, WV 26506

WISCONSIN

OLLI at University of Wisconsin-Milwaukee
Milwaukee, WI 53211

WYOMING

OLLI at Casper College, 125 College Drive, Casper, WY 82601

Degree-Seeking Seniors

There are over 10,000 colleges and universities that provide reduced or free tuition for senior citizens. Since each college sets its own criteria, the minimum age to qualify may be as low as 50, or as high as 65. It's best to use this section as encouragement that your local colleges *probably* have programs, even if they are unadvertised and difficult to find. If the local college doesn't offer senior citizens free tuition, ask them to start! Senior citizens bring life experience and diversity to a classroom unlike any other demographic.

The following states require public colleges to offer full tuition waivers to degree-seeking senior citizens.

Alabama
All community colleges in the state if you are over age 60.

Alaska
All public colleges in the state if you collect social security.

Arkansas
All public colleges in the state if you are over age 60.

Connecticut
All public colleges in the state if you are over age 62.

Delaware
All public colleges in the state if you are over age 60.

Florida
All public colleges in the state if you are over age 60.

Georgia
All public colleges in the state if you are over age 60.

Illinois
All public colleges in the state if you are over age 65.

Indiana
All public colleges in the state if you are over age 60.

Kentucky
All public colleges in the state if you are over age 65.

Maine
All public colleges in the state if you are over age 65.

Maryland
All public colleges in the state if you are over age 60.

Massachusetts
All public colleges in the state if you are over age 60.

Minnesota
All public colleges in the state for senior citizens.

Missouri
All public colleges in the state if you are over age 65.

Montana
All public colleges in the state if you are over age 65.

New Jersey
All public colleges in the state if you are over age 60.

New Mexico

All public colleges in the state if you are over age 65. ($5.00 per credit fee)

North Carolina

All public colleges in the state if you are over age 65.

Rhode Island

All public colleges in the state if you are over age 60.

South Carolina

All public colleges in the state if you are over age 60.

8 FREE TUITION FOR MILITARY SERVICE

"Accept the challenges so that you may feel the exhilaration of victory."
–General George S. Patton

Unlike other sections of this book, you probably already know that "free education" is a common benefit in exchange for your service to our country. In fact, you may even know someone who has earned their degree using Tuition Assistance or the G.I. Bill program. Recruiters, soldiers, and veterans are very enthusiastic and very loyal to their branch of service. As such, asking questions about education benefits can become a recruiting effort, especially if you've not made up your mind to serve. In this chapter, we'll look only at the structure in which earning a tuition-free degree is possible. The considerations and decisions to serve are your own.

It is important to remember that each branch of the military is set up a little differently, and each have precise fitness, age, and admission criteria for different occupations. Be sure to investigate your eligibility early in your consideration process. This section should be used as a jump off point. You can delve into the finer details once you've settled on a branch, and taken your Armed Services Vocational Aptitude Battery test (ASVAB). Your ASVAB test score, not personal preference, determines the jobs or Military Occupational Specialties (MOS) you'll be eligible to train for. The training you receive, and the college credit that follows, will be based on your MOS assignment. If you're currently serving, be sure to contact your unit's education services officer.

Note: *I use the term "soldier" to include all service members in all branches.*

Official websites of our armed forces
(Notice that these are **not** *dot com* web addresses)

Air Force:	www.af.mil
Air Force Reserves:	www.afrc.af.mil
Army:	www.army.mil
Army Reserves:	www.usar.army.mil
Coast Guard:	www.uscg.mil
Coast Guard Reserves:	reserve.uscg.mil
Marine Corps:	www.marines.mil
Marine Corps Reserves:	www.marforres.marines.mil
Navy:	www.navy.mil
Navy Reserves:	www.navyreserve.navy.mil
Veterans:	www.benefits.va.gov

Earning a degree in the military isn't as straightforward as some other paths, simply because how and where you "start" determines some of the variables that you'll encounter as you work toward your degree. Furthermore, each of these paths will take you to a degree, but some make better use of your benefits in the process. In this chapter, we'll explore tuition-free degree opportunities for enlisted soldiers, aspiring officers, and veterans. For those just learning the terminology: enlisted soldiers are the military's work force, the officers manage the enlisted soldiers, and veterans are former soldiers or officers.

Earning a Degree While You're Enlisted

Enlisted service members make up the bulk of our military in every branch of the armed forces. Like civilian industries, enlisted soldiers can get promoted through hard work, time served, and by earning a college degree. Though promotions and college degrees are not always a soldier's goal, the Department of Defense recognizes the value of higher education, and has established a relationship with the American Council on Education (ACE) to make this path as painless as possible.

While it's not widely known, every service member has a transcript from the moment they enter boot camp. This transcript, called a Joint Services Transcript (JST), tracks every formal educational activity from day 1 to separation. Boot Camp, for instance, is worth 4 college credits, and is recorded on their JST. In addition, the military occupation during their service will also involve training, and in most cases, will be worth potential college credit. Many soldiers know they can use their occupational credit (frequently called ACE credit) toward a degree *after* separation from the service, but earning a degree *during* your active service will squeeze thousands more dollars out of your education benefits.

Soldiers have access to Tuition Assistance, a benefit that pays 100% of undergraduate tuition up to $250 per semester hour ($166 per quarter hour) while on active duty. This benefit dissolves when the soldier separates from the service, and can't be retained for future use. In other words, if you don't use it, you'll lose it. An important aspect of Tuition Assistance, is that it is completely separate from the soldier's GI Bill benefit. Many colleges advertise "no out of pocket cost to soldiers" but what they don't reveal is that they'll require you to dip into your GI Bill, apply for scholarships, or seek out federal loans and grants. Resourceful planning allows you to seek a degree during service that uses only your Tuition Assistance, and saves your GI Bill for later.

All branches dictate a specific number of dollars or credits a soldier is entitled to use each year. To make up the deficiency of credit, the soldier can use a free credit by exam testing option called CLEP or DSST. These are multiple choice college credit-awarding exams that any soldier can attempt. There is no limit to the number of exam credits a soldier can earn.

For those serving in the Air Force, airmen have the option of completing an entire Associates of Science Degree through the Community College of the Air Force (CCAF). With a choice of 70 different degrees over 5 fields of study, these degrees are designed to align precisely with their Military Occupation Specialty training/technical credit. This program leaves only 5 general education courses for the soldier to complete, and those are paid for using Tuition Assistance or free credit by exam testing (CLEP or DSST) options.

To facilitate earning a bachelor's degree, the Air Force created a special program called Air University Associates to Bachelor's Cooperation (AU-ABC). 71 Participating colleges guarantee transfer of the airman's associate degree earned through the CCAF into a bachelor's degree program, leaving only 60 credits toward completion. Like other service members, Tuition Assistance then pays 100% up to $250 per credit hour ($166 per quarter hour) toward the remaining credits. If you separate from the military before your degree is complete, you must switch to your GI Bill for funding, but it is possible to complete a full associate's degree and a full bachelor's degree using Tuition Assistance while serving active or reserve in any branch.

Selecting a Military-Favorable College While You're Enlisted

Though it may have been difficult for enlisted soldiers to pursue a degree in the past, colleges now cater directly to our military through distance learning initiatives, the use of eTextbooks, and other methods that do not require a soldier to be in a physical location. The Department of Defense maintains a database of colleges that are approved to participate in Tuition Assistance. Currently, 2,708 colleges operating at over 12,000 locations are approved. It's up to the soldier to choose, apply, and enroll in an approved degree program. As a civilian, you might not have access to an official list, but you can access an unofficial one at www.dodmou.com.

While researching for this book, I quickly discovered that weeding through the list of 12,000 approved colleges wasn't something our soldiers had time to do. I created a bullet-proof list that uses very specific criteria to ensure that every enlisted soldier in every branch could earn a full degree for no tuition out of pocket. I've checked each college's accreditation, admissions policy, and acceptance of non-traditional credit like CLEP and DSST exams.

Every college on the Military-Favorable Colleges list meets *all* of the following criteria:

1) The college appears on the Department of Defense Voluntary Education Partnership Memorandum of Understanding list.
2) The college qualifies as an AU-ABC school for Community College of the Air Force graduates.
3) The tuition cost is priced at or under the Tuition Assistance limit of $250.00 per semester hour or $166 per quarter hour for 2015-2016.*
4) A full associate's and or bachelor's degree can be earned at the college.
5) All courses required for the degree are offered by the college through distance learning.
6) The college must award credit for a soldier's ACE-evaluated military job training credit (amounts vary).
7) The college must award credit for passing CLEP and DSST exams, and must accept at least 12 credits.
8) The college must be regionally accredited**

Always check the cost per credit. Colleges can charge more than the TA cap and still advertise "no out of pocket costs" by signing you up for a student loan, scholarship, or using your GI Bill.

** *Be aware that many DOD and AU-ABC approved colleges are not regionally accredited, which may be a barrier to civilian employment or graduate school admissions later on. Only regionally accredited colleges are included in this list. Check any college's current accreditation status using the United States Department of Education Accreditation Database.*
http://ope.ed.gov/accreditation

MILITARY-FAVORABLE COLLEGES

American Military University
111 West Congress Street
Charles Town, WV 25414
877-777-9081
www.amu.apus.edu
Type: Private For-Profit Distance Learning University
Religious affiliation: None
U.S. News & World Report National Rank: Unranked
SAT /ACT requirement for soldiers: None
Acceptance rate for soldiers: 100%
CLEP / DSST acceptance policy: 15 credits toward an associate degree, 30 credits toward a bachelor's degree
Transfer credit acceptance policy: Up to 75% of the degree
Free undergraduate options: Distance learning (22 associate degrees, 42 bachelor degrees)
Other: Textbooks are included at no additional charge.

Amridge University
1200 Taylor Road
Montgomery, AL 36117
(334) 387-3877
www.amridgeuniversity.edu
Type: Private Non-Profit Distance Learning University
Religious affiliation: Churches of Christ
U.S. News & World Report National Rank: Unranked
SAT /ACT requirement for soldiers: None
Acceptance rate for soldiers: 100%
CLEP / DSST acceptance policy: 12 credits toward a degree
Transfer credit acceptance policy: Up to 80 credits
Free undergraduate options: Distance learning (1 associate degree, 10 bachelor degrees)

Ashford University
8620 Spectrum Center Boulevard
San Diego, CA 92123-1406
Phone: 866-475-0317
www.ashford.edu
Type: Private For-Profit Distance Learning University
Religious affiliation: None
U.S. News & World Report National Rank: Unranked
SAT /ACT requirement for soldiers: None
Acceptance rate for soldiers: 100%
CLEP / DSST acceptance policy: Generous
Transfer credit acceptance policy: Up to 90 credits
Free undergraduate options: Distance learning (2 associate degrees, 11 bachelor degrees)

Bellevue University
1000 Galvin Road South
Bellevue, NE 68005
800.756.7920
www.bellevue.edu
Type: Private For-Profit Distance Learning University
Religious affiliation: None
U.S. News & World Report National Rank: Unranked
SAT /ACT requirement for soldiers: None
Acceptance rate for soldiers: 100%
CLEP / DSST acceptance policy: unlimited credits toward a bachelor's degree
Transfer credit acceptance policy: Up to 75% of the degree
Free undergraduate options: Distance learning (5 bachelor degrees)
Other: military saturation is >40% of student body

Bismarck State College

P.O. Box 5587

Bismarck, ND 58506-5587

Phone: 701-224-5400

www.bismarckstate.edu

Type: Public Non-Profit University

Religious affiliation: None

U.S. News & World Report National Rank: #69 Midwest Region

SAT /ACT requirement for soldiers: None

Acceptance rate for soldiers: 100%

CLEP / DSST acceptance policy: Up to 45 credits

Transfer credit acceptance policy: Up to 90 credits

Free undergraduate options: Distance learning (20 associate degrees)

Brandman University

16355 Laguna Canyon Road

Irvine, CA 92618

Phone: 949-341-9800

www.brandman.edu

Type: Private Non-Profit Distance Learning University

Religious affiliation: None

U.S. News & World Report National Rank: Unranked

SAT /ACT requirement for soldiers: None

Acceptance rate for soldiers: 100%

CLEP / DSST acceptance policy: Generous

Transfer credit acceptance policy: Up to 96 credits

Free undergraduate options: Distance learning (1 associate degree, 34 bachelor degrees)

DeVry University (multiple campus locations)

One Tower Lane

Oakbrook Terrace, IL 60181-4264

Phone: 630-571-7700

www.devry.edu

Type: Private For-Profit University

Religious affiliation: None

U.S. News & World Report National Rank: Unranked

SAT /ACT requirement for soldiers: None

Acceptance rate: 100%

Acceptance category: Open enrollment

CLEP / DSST acceptance policy: Generous

Transfer credit acceptance policy: Up to 90 credits

Free undergraduate options: Distance learning (5 associate degrees, 73 bachelor degrees)

Excelsior College

7 Columbia Circle

Albany, NY 12203-5159

888-647-2388

www.excelsior.edu

Type: Private Non-Profit Distance Learning College

Religious affiliation: None

U.S. News & World Report National Rank: Unranked

SAT /ACT requirement for soldiers: None

Acceptance rate for soldiers: 100%

CLEP acceptance policy: unlimited credits toward an associate or bachelor's degree

Transfer credit acceptance policy: Generous

Free undergraduate options: Distance learning (15 associate degrees, 55 bachelor degrees)

Kaplan University (multiple campus locations)
1801 E Kimberly Rd Ste 1
Davenport, IA 52807
Phone: 563-355-3500
www.kaplanuniversity.edu
Type: Private For-Profit Distance Learning University
Religious affiliation: None
U.S. News & World Report National Rank: Unranked
SAT /ACT requirement for soldiers: None
Acceptance rate for soldiers: 100%
CLEP / DSST acceptance policy: Generous
Transfer credit acceptance policy: Up to 75% of degree
Free undergraduate options: Distance learning (13 associate degrees and 4 bachelor's degrees directly tied to occupational training, other degrees available.)

Liberty University
1971 University Blvd
Lynchburg, VA 24502
Phone: 434-582-2000
www.liberty.edu
Type: Private Non-Profit Christian University
Religious affiliation: Christian
U.S. News & World Report National Rank: #80 Regional
SAT /ACT requirement for soldiers: None
Acceptance rate for soldiers: 100%
CLEP / DSST acceptance policy: Generous
Transfer credit acceptance policy: Up to 75% of degree
Free undergraduate options: Distance learning (12 associate degrees and 58 bachelor degrees under Service member Opportunity College agreement, non-SOC degrees also available.)

Saint Leo University
33701 State Road 52
Saint Leo, FL 33574
Phone: 352-588-8200
www.ashford.edu
Type: Private Non-Profit University
Religious affiliation: Catholic
U.S. News & World Report National Rank: Unranked
SAT /ACT requirement for soldiers: None
Acceptance rate for soldiers: 100%
CLEP / DSST acceptance policy: up to 30 credits
Transfer credit acceptance policy: varies based on degree,
approximately 15 Saint Leo credits required.
Free undergraduate options: Distance learning   (4 associate
degrees, 16 bachelor degrees)

Southwestern College
100 College Street
Winfield, KS 67156-2499
Phone: 800-846-1543
www.sckans.edu
Type: Private Non-Profit University
Religious affiliation: United Methodist Church
U.S. News & World Report National Rank: #84 (Regional)
SAT /ACT requirement for soldiers: None
Acceptance rate for soldiers: 100%
CLEP / DSST acceptance policy: Generous
Transfer credit acceptance policy: up to 94 credits in transfer, 30
Southwestern credits required. Transfer of AA or AS degree meets
general education requirement.
Free undergraduate options: Distance learning   (17 bachelor
degrees)

Strayer University (Multiple campus locations)
1133 15th St NW
Washington, DC 20005
Phone: 202-408-2400
www.strayer.edu
Type: Private For-Profit Distance Learning University
Religious affiliation: None
U.S. News & World Report National Rank: Unranked
SAT /ACT requirement for soldiers: None
Acceptance rate for soldiers: 100%
CLEP / DSST acceptance policy: Generous
Transfer credit acceptance policy: Up to 84 quarter credits
Free undergraduate options: Distance learning (7 associate degrees, 7 bachelor degrees)

SUNY- Empire State College
2 Union Ave.
Saratoga Springs, NY 12866
Phone: 800-847-3000
www.sec.edu
Type: Public non-Profit University
Religious affiliation: None
U.S. News & World Report National Rank: Unranked
SAT /ACT requirement for soldiers: None
Acceptance rate for soldiers: 100%
CLEP / DSST acceptance policy: Generous. This college awards 16 credits for a score of 70 on a foreign language exam. This is noteworthy, as it exceeds ACE recommendations.
Transfer credit acceptance policy: Up to 40 credits toward an associates, 93 credits toward a bachelor's degree.
Free undergraduate options: Distance learning (12 areas of study)

Thomas Edison State College
101 W State Street
Trenton, NJ 08608
(888) 442-8372
www.tesc.edu
Type: Public Non-Profit State College
Religious affiliation: None
U.S. News & World Report National Rank: Unranked
SAT /ACT requirement for soldiers: None
Acceptance rate for soldiers: 100%
CLEP acceptance policy: unlimited credits toward an associate or bachelor's degree
Transfer credit acceptance policy: Generous
Free undergraduate options: Distance learning (8 associate degrees, 28 bachelor degrees)

Troy University
University Avenue
Troy, AL 36082-0001
Phone: 334-670-3100
www.troy.edu
Type: Public Non-Profit University
Religious affiliation: None
U.S. News & World Report National Rank: Unranked
SAT /ACT requirement for soldiers: None
Acceptance rate for soldiers: 100%
CLEP / DSST acceptance policy: Generous
Transfer credit acceptance policy: No limit
Free undergraduate options: Distance learning (14 associate degrees, 30 bachelor degrees)

University of the Incarnate Word
4301 Broadway
San Antonio, TX 78209
Phone: 210-829-6000
http://military.uiw.edu
Type: Private Non-Profit University
Religious affiliation: Catholic
U.S. News & World Report National Rank: #63 Regional
SAT /ACT requirement for soldiers: None
Acceptance rate for soldiers: 100%
CLEP / DSST acceptance policy: up to 30 credits
Transfer credit acceptance policy: Up to 75 credits
Free undergraduate options: Distance learning (9 associate degrees, 22 bachelor degrees)
Other: Textbooks are included at no additional charge.

University of Phoenix
1625 Fountainhead Parkway
Tempe, AZ 85282
Phone: 480-804-7600
www.phoenix.edu
Type: Private For-Profit University
Religious affiliation: None
U.S. News & World Report National Rank: Unranked
SAT /ACT requirement for soldiers: None
Acceptance rate for soldiers: 100%
CLEP / DSST acceptance policy: Generous
Transfer credit acceptance policy: Up to 90 credits
Free undergraduate options: Distance learning (28 associate degrees, 80 bachelor degrees)

Wilmington University

320 DuPont Highway

New Castle, DE 19720

Phone: 302-328-9401

www.wilmu.edu

Type: Private For-Profit Distance Learning University

Religious affiliation: None

U.S. News & World Report National Rank: Unranked

SAT /ACT requirement for soldiers: >450 each section of SAT or Accuplacer exam

Acceptance rate for soldiers: 99%

CLEP / DSST acceptance policy: Generous

Transfer credit acceptance policy: Up to 75 credits

Free undergraduate options: Distance learning   (2 associate degrees, 23 bachelor degrees)

Aspiring Military Officers

For those aiming to become a commissioned officer, earning a degree is part of that process. We'll explore the four paths to becoming an officer that can be completed tuition-free.

1) Enlisted soldier completes his degree using Tuition Assistance while serving. Upon graduation, the soldier may apply to their branch's officer training program (no cost).
2) Attend Military Academy. Military Academy graduates enter the service as a commissioned officer with a Bachelor's of Science degree in hand. Though the competition for admission is exceptionally competitive, all are tuition-free, cover living expenses, and provide a cash stipend to the student. ROTC is required as a component of each academy.
3) Civilian ROTC. A civilian ROTC is a voluntary program that is housed in a civilian college. ROTC programs exist at both community colleges and four year colleges. ROTC students receive full tuition scholarships. Most ROTC colleges also cover room, board, and a monthly cash stipend to the student.
4) Health Professions Scholarships through the Army, Navy, and Air Force pay 100% of the student's medical, dental, advanced practice nursing, optometry, pharmacy, veterinary, social worker, or physician assistant tuition. Candidates must already possess a bachelor's degree.

MILITARY ACADEMIES (ROTC)

United States Air Force Academy
HQ USAFA/RRS, 2304 Cadet Drive, Suite 2300, USAF Academy, CO 80840
(800) 443-9266
www.usafa.af.mil
Type: Military Academy
U.S. News & World Report National Rank: #27 (National) #5 (Undergraduate Engineering) #62 (Undergraduate Business)
Regular admissions: At least 17 but not 23 years of age, unmarried, no dependents, SAT or ACT, interview, High School Diploma or GED. Applicant must also obtain nomination from a U.S. Senator or U.S. Representative, the Vice President of the U.S., the President of the United States, or other specialized category. Physical health and fitness standards required.
Homeschool admissions: Detailed curriculum descriptions required. Full criteria outlined in "Advice to Homeschool Applicants" Air Force booklet.
SAT requirement: mid to high 600's/ **ACT requirement:** 30
Acceptance rate: 15.4% / **Acceptance category:** Competitive
CLEP acceptance policy: No
AP acceptance policy: Score of 4 or more plus verification using Air Force exam to earn credit
Transfer credit acceptance policy: Considered
Housing: Yes/ **Co-ed housing:** Yes
Athletic programs: Yes
Free undergraduate options: Campus bachelors only, 27 majors
What's free? 100% tuition, room, board, meal plan, and books. Cadets earn monthly pay.
Service requirement: Upon graduation, serve as a commissioned officer in the Air Force for at least 8 years.

United States Coast Guard Academy

31 MOHEGAN AVENUE, NEW LONDON, CT 06320

800-883-8724

www.cga.edu

Type: Military Academy

U.S. News & World Report National Rank: #1 (Regional) #12 (Undergraduate Engineering)

Regular admissions: At least 17 but not 23 years of age, SAT or ACT, High School Diploma or GED. Physical health and fitness standards required. Special nomination is not required.

Homeschool admissions: no difference, community college coursework suggested

SAT requirement: No minimum. >1100 combined suggested

ACT requirement: No minimum. >24 suggested

Acceptance rate: 16.5%/

Acceptance category: Competitive

CLEP acceptance policy: No

AP acceptance policy: No

Transfer credit acceptance policy: Yes. Credit granted does not reduce length of curriculum

Housing: Yes/

Co-ed housing: Yes

Athletic programs: Yes

Free undergraduate options: Campus bachelors only, 13 majors

What's free? 100% tuition, room, board, meal plan, and books. Cadets earn monthly pay.

Service requirement: Upon graduation, commissioned ensigns are obligated to serve at least 5 years.

United States Merchant Marine Academy

300 Steamboat Rd, Great Neck, NY 11024

(516) 773-5258

www.usmma.edu

Type: Military Academy

U.S. News & World Report National Rank: #3 (Regional) #29 (Undergraduate Engineering)

Regular admissions: At least 17 but not 23 years of age, unmarried, no dependents, SAT or ACT, interview, High School Diploma or GED. Applicant must also obtain nomination from a U.S. Senator or U.S. Representative from the applicant's state of residence. Physical health and fitness standards required.

Homeschool admissions: No difference.

SAT requirement: >560

ACT requirement: >24

Acceptance rate: 18.2%

Acceptance category: Competitive

CLEP acceptance policy: No

AP acceptance policy: No

Transfer credit acceptance policy: No

Housing: Yes

Co-ed housing: Yes

Athletic programs: Yes

Free undergraduate options: Campus bachelors only, 5 majors

What's free? 100% tuition, room, board, meal plan, and books.

Service requirement: Graduates can choose to work 5 years in the U.S. maritime industry with 8 years of service as an officer in any reserve unit of the armed forces or 5 years active duty in any of the nation's armed forces.

United States Military Academy

West Point, NY

(845) 938-4011

www.usma.edu

Type: Military Academy

U.S. News & World Report National Rank:

Regular admissions: At least 17 but not 22 years of age, unmarried, no dependents, SAT or ACT, interview, High School Diploma or GED. Applicant must also obtain nomination from a U.S. Senator or U.S. Representative, the Vice President of the U.S., or the President of the United States. Physical health and fitness standards required.

Homeschool admissions:

SAT requirement: >600

ACT requirement: >25

Acceptance rate: 9%

Acceptance category: Elite/exceptionally competitive

CLEP acceptance policy: No

AP acceptance policy: No

Transfer credit acceptance policy: No

Housing: Yes

Co-ed housing: Yes

Athletic programs: Yes

Free undergraduate options: Campus bachelors only, 36 majors

What's free? 100% tuition, room, board, meal plan, and books. Cadets earn monthly pay.

Service requirement: Upon graduation, you will be commissioned as a second lieutenant in the Army and serve for five years on active duty (if you choose to depart the Army after five years, you will be required to serve three years in the Inactive Ready Reserve).

United States Naval Academy

121 Blake Road, Annapolis, MD 21402
(410) 293-1000
www.usna.edu
Type: Military Academy
U.S. News & World Report National Rank: #13 (National) #6 (Undergraduate Engineering)
Regular admissions: At least 17 but not 23 years of age, unmarried, no dependents, SAT or ACT, interview, High School Diploma or GED. Applicant must also obtain nomination from a U.S. Senator or U.S. Representative, the Vice President of the U.S., or the President of the United States. Physical health and fitness standards required.
Homeschool admissions: Detailed curriculum descriptions required.
SAT requirement: mid 600's
ACT requirement: high 20's
Acceptance rate: 7.4%
Acceptance category: Elite/exceptionally competitive
CLEP acceptance policy: No
AP acceptance policy: score of 4 or more
Transfer credit acceptance policy: No
Housing: Yes
Co-ed housing: Yes
Athletic programs: Yes
Free undergraduate options: Campus bachelors only, 26 majors
What's free? 100% tuition, room, board, meal plan, and books. Cadets earn monthly pay.
Service requirement: 5 years active duty service required upon graduation.

CIVILIAN ACADEMIES (ROTC)

There are currently more than 1,100 participating two and four-year colleges in the Reserve Officer Training Corps (ROTC). Students enrolled in ROTC programs receive full tuition scholarships toward their degree and officer training at the same time. Most ROTC programs also provide scholarships that cover room, board, and a monthly cash stipend to the student. Your branch and enlistment preference (active or reserve), will determine your service obligation upon completion. See each branch's current database of participating programs and criteria.

ARMY
http://www.goarmy.com/rotc.html

NAVY
http://www.nrotc.navy.mil

AIR FORCE
https://www.afrotc.com

MARINES
Use Navy ROTC program

U.S. COAST GUARD (Active and Reserve)
(Does not offer ROTC) See: College Student Pre-Commissioning Initiative

HEALTH PROFESSIONS SCHOLARSHIP

As an incentive offered through the Army, Navy, and Air Force, students pursuing professional health degrees (masters or doctorate) are eligible for 100% tuition waivers. Different branches offer additional incentives. During professional training, the student is placed on inactive reserve, and upon graduation, will begin their service obligation. Candidates in this program must already hold an accredited bachelor's degree and have received acceptance into graduate school

ARMY
What's free? 100% tuition, textbooks, lab and fees
Cash stipend: $2,000 per month
Sign on bonus: $20,000
Qualifying degrees: medicine MD or DO, dentistry, veterinary science, pharmacy, nursing, optometry or psychology
Eligibility: Bachelor's degree. Currently enrolled or letter of acceptance into graduate program. Must qualify as a commissioned officer.
Service requirement: 1-year of active duty service for every year of scholarship received.

NAVY
What's free? 100% tuition, textbooks, lab and fees
Cash stipend: $2,000 per month
Sign on bonus: $20,000
Qualifying degrees: medicine MD or DO, dentistry, veterinary science, pharmacy, nursing, optometry or psychology
Eligibility: Bachelor's degree. Currently enrolled or letter of acceptance into graduate program. Must qualify as a commissioned officer.
Service requirement: 4 years of active duty service following residency.

AIR FORCE

What's free? 100% tuition, textbooks, lab and fees

Cash stipend: $2,000 per month

Sign on bonus: $20,000

Qualifying degrees: medicine, dentistry, veterinary science, pharmacy, nursing, optometry or psychology

Eligibility: Bachelor's degree. Currently enrolled or letter of acceptance into graduate program. Must qualify as a commissioned officer.

Service requirement: 1-year of active duty service for every year of scholarship received.

VETERANS

The United States Department of Veteran Affairs, www.va.gov, is the first point of contact for any veteran. The VA will help you determine your eligibility, which type of GI Bill program is your best option, and how to choose a qualifying school. Furthermore, if you qualify for state benefits, and they'll explain those options to you.

If you'd like to get a general idea of your benefits before contacting the VA, you can use the free online GI Bill Comparison Tool. **http://department-of-veterans-affairs.github.io/gi-bill-comparison-tool.** By entering in your military status and length of service, you'll instantly be able to compare GI Bill benefit options for every approved college in the country. Knowing your benefits ensures that you'll make the best decisions for you and your family. You can also search for colleges that participate in Yellow Ribbon Scholarships, Principles of Excellence (POE), and other specialized benefits. If you served before 9/11, your benefits will differ from those who served after 9/11, needless to say, it's important to get VA information directly from your Veterans Affairs office.

9 FREE TUITION STUDYING ABROAD

"Adventure is worthwhile."
—Aesop

For many students, a study abroad program is the highlight of their academic career. Exposure to diverse cultures, developing independence, and an opportunity to learn a new language are popular reasons students pursue these programs. When an American student studies abroad, they're paying college tuition to their American university, plus expenses for that semester. It's generally very expensive, plus, scholarships and grants typically don't cover study abroad semesters.

What few students know is that they can skip enrollment at an American university and enroll directly in a degree program outside the United States. American students can complete entire degree programs, taught in English, tuition-free! While tuition in the United States continues to rise, many countries are eliminating tuition altogether, and opening their doors to all students, national and foreign.

The universities in this chapter are considered "comparable" to American universities in quality and accreditation, but beware that certain fields (medicine, nursing, dentistry, etc.) may place restrictions on degrees earned outside of the United States, so when in doubt, check it out.

Many universities in this section offer degrees taught in English that are not free, and many offer degrees for free that are not taught in English. So for simplicity, the selections in this chapter list only full degree programs that are both free and in English.

Jennifer's Tip: *If you're considering international study, use the university's official website.*

ARGENTINA

University of Buenos Aires
Address: Viamonte 430, 1053, Buenos Aires, Argentina
Phone: +54 11 4510-1100
University Website: www.uba.ar
Official Country Website: www.argentina.gob.ar
Type: Public University
Dominant Language: Spanish
Courses taught in English: Yes, though basic Spanish is suggested.
What's free? Tuition (100 majors)
What's not? Living expenses/housing
Eligibility: High School diploma.
Housing: International dorms, Argentinian host family, private apartment
Notable information: Largest and top ranked university in Argentina.

BRAZIL

Federal University of Rio de Janeiro

Address: Ave. Pedro Calmon, 550 - Cidade Universitária, Rio de Janeiro - RJ, 21941-901, Brazil

Phone: +55 21 3938-9600

University Website: www.ufrj.br

Official Country Website: www.brasil.gov.br

Type: Public University

Dominant Language: Portuguese

Courses taught in English: Yes, though basic Portuguese is suggested.

What's free? Tuition (139 majors)

What's not? Living expenses/housing

Eligibility: Passport, letter of recommendation

Housing: private apartment

Notable information: Largest federal university in Brazil.

ESTONIA

University of Tartu
Address: Ülikooli 18, 50090 Tartu, Estonia
Phone: +372 737 5100
University Website: www.ut.ee
Official Country Education Website: www.studyinestonia.ee
Type: Public University
Dominant Language: Estonian
Courses taught in English: Yes. Business degree fully in English.
What's free? Tuition
What's not? Living expenses/housing
Eligibility: High school diploma
Housing: student dormitory
Notable information: Largest and top ranked university in Estonia.

Tallinn University of Technology
Address: 5, Tallinn, Estonia
Phone: +372 620 2002
University Website: www.ttu.ee/en
Official Country Education Website: www.studyinestonia.ee
Type: Public Technical University
Dominant Language: Estonian
Courses taught in English: Yes.
What's free? Tuition for Bachelors of Science in Engineering.
What's not? Living expenses/housing
Eligibility: Student must enroll full time, program is 3 years.
Housing: student dormitory
Notable information: The only technical university in Estonia. 21 degrees taught in English, but only 1 is free.

FINLAND

Aalto University
Address: Lönnrotinkatu 5, 50100 Mikkeli Finland
Phone: +358-50-4389837
University Website: www.aalto.fi
Official Country Education Website: www.studyinfinland.fi
Type: Public
Dominant Language: Finnish and Swedish
Courses taught in English: Yes (International Business undergraduate, more than 50 graduate degrees)
What's free? Tuition
What's not? Living expenses/housing
Eligibility: Hold educational certificates (diploma/GED) that make you eligible to apply for higher education in your home country, fulfill the language skills requirements.

Arcadia University of Applied Sciences
Address: Jan-Magnus Janssonin aukio 1, 00560 Helsinki, Finland
Phone: +358 20 7699699
University Website: www.arcada.fi
Official Country Education Website: www.studyinfinland.fi
Type: Public
Dominant Language: Finnish and Swedish
Courses taught in English: Yes (International Business, Marketing, Tourism, Materials and Processing Technology, Nursing, graduate degrees available)
What's free? Tuition
What's not? Living expenses/housing
Eligibility: Hold educational certificates (diploma/GED) that make you eligible to apply for higher education in your home country, fulfill the language skills requirements.

FINLAND

Centria University of Applied Sciences
Address: Ondegatan 2, 67100 Karleby, Finland
Phone: +358 6 8250000
University Website: www.centria.fi
Official Country Education Website: www.studyinfinland.fi
Type: Private
Dominant Language: Finnish and Swedish
Courses taught in English: Yes (Business Management, Chemistry and Technology, Information Technology, Nursing, Industrial Management)
What's free? Tuition
What's not? Living expenses/housing
Eligibility: Hold educational certificates (diploma/GED) that make you eligible to apply for higher education in your home country, fulfill the language skills requirements.

Haaga-Helia University of Applied Sciences
Address: Hietakummuntie 1 A, 00700 Helsinki, Finland
Phone: +358 9 229611
University Website: www.haaga-helia.fi
Official Country Education Website: www.studyinfinland.fi
Type: Private
Dominant Language: Finnish and Swedish
Courses taught in English: Yes (International Business, International Sales and Marketing, Business Information Technology, Sports Studies, Tourism, Catering, Graduate degrees available)
What's free? Tuition
What's not? Living expenses/housing
Eligibility: Hold educational certificates (diploma/GED) that make you eligible to apply for higher education in your home country, fulfill the language skills requirements.

FINLAND

Helsinki Metropolia University of Applied Sciences
Address: Vanha maantie 6, 02650 Espoo, Finland
Phone: +358 9 74245000
University Website: www.metropolia.fi
Official Country Education Website: www.studyinfinland.fi
Type: Public
Dominant Language: Finnish and Swedish
Courses taught in English: Yes (Electronics, Environmental Engineering, European Business, Information Technology, International Business, Nursing, Social Services, Sustainable Building Engineering, and Graduate degrees available)
What's free? Tuition
What's not? Living expenses/housing
Eligibility: Hold educational certificates (diploma/GED) that make you eligible to apply for higher education in your home country, fulfill the language skills requirements.
Noteworthy: Finland's largest University of Applied Science.

Lahti University of Applied Sciences
Address: Niemenkatu 73, FI-15140 Lahti, Finland
Phone: +358-44-7081386
University Website: www.lamk.fi
Official Country Education Website: www.studyinfinland.fi
Type: Public
Dominant Language: Finnish and Swedish
Courses taught in English: Yes
What's free? Tuition (Nursing, Business Information Technology, International Business, Graduate degrees available)
What's not? Living expenses/housing
Eligibility: Hold educational certificates (diploma/GED) that make you eligible to apply for higher education in your home country, fulfill the language skills requirements.

FINLAND

Laurea University of Applied Sciences
Address: Vanha maantie 9, 02650 Espoo, Finland
Phone: +358 9 88687400
University Website: www.laurea.fi
Official Country Education Website: www.studyinfinland.fi
Type: Public
Dominant Language: Finnish and Swedish
Courses taught in English: Yes (Business Information Technology, Business Management, Nursing, Restaurant Entrepreneurship, Security Management, Social Services, and graduate degrees available)
What's free? Tuition
What's not? Living expenses/housing
Eligibility: Hold educational certificates (diploma/GED) that make you eligible to apply for higher education in your home country, fulfill the language skills requirements.

Mikkeli University of Applied Sciences
Address: Patteristonkatu 3, 50100 Mikkeli, Finland
Phone: +358 40 5345127
University Website: www.mamk.fi
Official Country Education Website: www.studyinfinland.fi
Type: Public
Dominant Language: Finnish and Swedish
Courses taught in English: Yes
What's free? Tuition (Business Management, Environmental Engineering, Information Technology)
What's not? Living expenses/housing
Eligibility: Hold educational certificates (diploma/GED) that make you eligible to apply for higher education in your home country, fulfill the language skills requirements.

FINLAND

Novia University of Applied Sciences
Address: Sarjakatu 2, 65230 Vaasa, Finland
Phone: +358 6 3285000
University Website: www.novia.fi
Official Country Education Website: www.studyinfinland.fi
Type: Public
Dominant Language: Finnish and Swedish
Courses taught in English: Yes (Maritime Management, Maritime Technology, Sustainable Coastal Management, Nursing, and Graduate degrees available)
What's free? Tuition
What's not? Living expenses/housing
Eligibility: Hold educational certificates (diploma/GED) that make you eligible to apply for higher education in your home country, fulfill the language skills requirements.

GERMANY

Bonn-Rhine-Sieg University of Applied Sciences
Address: Grantham-Allee 20, 53757 Sankt Augustin, Germany
Phone: +49 2241 8650
University Website: https://www.h-brs.de
Official Country Education Website: www.daad.de/en
Dominant Language: German
Courses taught in English: Yes (Applied Biology, Graduate degrees available)
What's free? Tuition
What's not? Living expenses/housing

GERMANY

Darmstadt University of Applied Sciences
Address: Haardtring 100, 64295 Darmstadt, Germany
Phone: +49 6151 160
University Website: www.h-da.de
Official Country Education Website: www.daad.de/en
Dominant Language: German
Courses taught in English: Yes (Animation and Game, Graduate degrees available)
What's free? Tuition
What's not? Living expenses/housing
Notable information: Selection criteria among most elite in Germany

Freie Universitat Berlin
Address: Kaiserswerther Str. 16-18, 14195 Berlin, Germany
Phone: +49 30 8381
University Website: www.fu-berlin.de
Official Country Education Website: www.daad.de/en
Dominant Language: German
Courses taught in English: Yes, though basic German is suggested.
What's free? Tuition
What's not? Living expenses/housing
Notable information: 1/3 of the students are international.

GERMANY

Heidelberg University
Address: Grabengasse 1, 69117 Heidelberg, Germany
Phone: +49 6221 540
University Website: www.uni-heidelberg.de
Official Country Education Website: www.daad.de/en
Dominant Language: German
Courses taught in English: Yes, though basic German is suggested. (Only International Business is taught in English)
What's free? Tuition
What's not? Living expenses/housing
Notable information: This is the oldest university in Germany and is ranked 55th in the world.

Hochschule Worms University of Applied Sciences
Address: Erenburgerstraße 19, 67549 Worms, Germany
Phone: +49 6241 5090
University Website: http://www.hs-worms.de/
Official Country Education Website: www.daad.de/en
Dominant Language: German
Courses taught in English: Yes (Aviation Management, Graduate degrees available)
What's free? Tuition
What's not? Living expenses/housing

GERMANY

Macromedia University of Applied Sciences for Media and Communication

Address: Gollierstraße 4, 80339 München, Germany
Phone: +49 89 5441510
University Website: www.macromedia-fachhochschule.de
Official Country Education Website: www.daad.de/en
Dominant Language: German
Courses taught in English: Yes (Design, Media, and Communication)
What's free? Tuition
What's not? Living expenses/housing
Notable information: Largest private media college in Germany.

Mainz University

Address: Saarstraße 21, 55122 Mainz, Germany
Phone: +49 6131 390
University Website: www.uni-mainz.de
Official Country Education Website: www.daad.de/en
Dominant Language: German
Courses taught in English: Yes (American Studies, British Studies, Graduate degrees available)
What's free? Tuition
What's not? Living expenses / housing

GERMANY

Rhine-Waal University of Applied Sciences
Address: Landwehr 4, 47533 Kleve, Germany
Phone: +49 2821 806730
University Website: www.hochschule-rhein-waal.de
Official Country Education Website: www.daad.de/en
Dominant Language: German
Courses taught in English: Yes (Ag Business, Bioengineering, Biomaterials Science, Electronics, Environment and Energy, Gender and Diversity, Industrial Engineering, Information Design, International Relations, International Tax Law, Mechanical Engineering, Mobility and Logistics, Graduate degrees available)
What's free? Tuition
What's not? Living expenses/housing

University of Leipzig
Address: Augustusplatz 10, 04109 Leipzig, Germany
Phone: +49 341 97108
University Website: www.zv.uni-leipzig.de
Official Country Education Website: www.daad.de/en
Dominant Language: German
Courses taught in English: Yes (Physics, English Studies, and American Studies)
What's free? Tuition
What's not? Living expenses/housing
Notable information: Second oldest university in Germany

GERMANY

Jacobs University Bremen
Address: Campus Ring 1, 28759 Bremen, Germany
Phone: +49 421 20040
University Website: www.jacobs-university.de
Official Country Education Website: www.daad.de/en
Dominant Language: German
Courses taught in English: All courses taught in English.
(Biochemistry and Cell Biology, Chemistry, Computer Science, Earth and Environmental Sciences, Electrical and Computer Engineering, Global Economics, Industrial Engineering, Integrated Social Sciences, Intelligent Mobile Systems, International Business, Mathematics, Medical Nature Science, Physics, Psychology, Graduate degrees available)
What's free? Tuition
What's not? Living expenses/housing
Notable information: All students live on the 80-acre campus. Jacobs University is a privately funded research university.

NORWAY

Oslo and Akershus University College of Applied Sciences
Address: Pilestredet 46, 0167 Oslo, Norway
Phone: +47 67 23 50 00
University Website: www.hioa.no
Dominant Language: Norwegian
Courses taught in English: Yes (Occupational Therapy and Graduate degrees available)
What's free? Tuition
What's not? Living expenses/housing
Eligibility: Students must apply through the Norwegian Universities and Colleges Admission Service.

NORWAY

University of Nordland
Address: Universitetsaleen 11, 8049 Bodø, Norway
Phone: +47 75 51 72 00
University Website: www.uin.no/en
Dominant Language: Norwegian
Courses taught in English: Yes (Animal Science, Northern Studies, Biology, and Graduate degrees available)
What's free? Tuition
What's not? Living expenses/housing
Eligibility: Students must apply through the Norwegian Universities and Colleges Admission Service

The University of Tromsø - The Arctic University of Norway
Address: Hansine Hansens veg 18, 9019 Tromsø, Norway
Phone: +47 77 64 40 00
University Website: https://uit.no
Dominant Language: Norwegian
Courses taught in English: Yes (Business Administration, Arctic Adventure Tourism, Biology, Rock and Roll Entrepreneurs, and Graduate degrees available.)
What's free? Tuition
What's not? Living expenses/housing
Eligibility: Students must apply through the Norwegian Universities and Colleges Admission Service

WATCH LIST

The following countries are on my watch list. These countries offer free tuition to their own citizens, and to foreigners, but only foreigners from certain countries such as the European Union. Currently, United States citizens are not eligible for free tuition in these countries, but these types of agreements are subject to change at any moment.

AUSTRIA
Free tuition for citizens of: Albania, Algeria, Armenia, Austria, Azerbaijan, Belarus, Belize, Bolivia, Bosnia and Herzegovina, Cameroon, China, Colombia, Congo, Costa Rica, Côte d'Ivoire, Croatia, Cuba, Dominican Republic, Ecuador, Egypt, El Salvador, Fiji, Georgia, Ghana, Guatemala, Guyana, Honduras, India, Indonesia, Iraq, Iran – Islamic Republic of Jamaica, Jordania, Kazakhstan, Kenia, Korea – People's Democratic Republic of Kosovo, Kyrgyzstan, Macedonia, Marshall Islands, Micronesia – Federated States of Moldova, Mongolia, Morocco, Namibia, Nicaragua, Nigeria, Niue, Pakistan, Palestinian, territories, Papua-New Guinea, Paraguay, Peru, Philippines, Saint Vincent and the Grenadines, Serbia and Montenegro, South Africa, Sri Lanka, Suriname, Swaziland, Syria – Arabian Republic of, Thailand, Taiwan, Tajikistan, Tokelau, Tonga, Tunisia, Turkmenistan, Ukraine, Uzbekistan, Vietnam, Wallis and Futuna, and Zimbabwe.

CHILE
Plans to begin offering free tuition by March 2016.

GREECE
Free tuition for citizens of: Austria, Belgium, Bulgaria, Croatia, Cyprus, the Czech Republic, Denmark, Estonia, Finland, France, Germany, Greece, Hungary, Ireland, Italy, Latvia, Lithuania, Luxembourg, Malta, the Netherlands, Poland, Portugal, Romania, Slovakia, Slovenia, Spain, Sweden, and the United Kingdom.

SWEDEN
Free tuition for citizens of: Austria, Belgium, Bulgaria, Croatia, Cyprus, the Czech Republic, Denmark, Estonia, Finland, France, Germany, Greece, Hungary, Ireland, Italy, Latvia, Lithuania, Luxembourg, Malta, the Netherlands, Poland, Portugal, Romania, Slovakia, Slovenia, Spain, Sweden, and the United Kingdom.

SLOVENIA
Free tuition for citizens of: Austria, Belgium, Bulgaria, Croatia, Cyprus, the Czech Republic, Denmark, Estonia, Finland, France, Germany, Greece, Hungary, Ireland, Italy, Latvia, Lithuania, Luxembourg, Malta, the Netherlands, Poland, Portugal, Romania, Slovakia, Slovenia, Spain, Sweden, and the United Kingdom.

Jennifer Cook - DeRosa

10 FREE TUITION BY OCCUPATION

"Never lose an opportunity of urging a practical beginning, however small, for it is wonderful how often in such matters the mustard-seed germinates and roots itself."
- Florence Nightingale

Federal government agencies identify careers and trade occupations that are important to our society or economy, and encourage enrollment through generous scholarship programs. These federal programs are technically scholarships, therefore can usually be used at **any** institution of the student's choosing, but admission to the university is also required. All of these scholarships pay tuition plus a stipend (salary) and are competitive.

CIVILIAN RESEARCH SCIENTIST or ENGINEER

Program Website: https://smart.asee.org
Program Title: SMART (Science, Mathematics And Research for Transformation)
Funding Source: Department of Defense
Eligibility: United States citizen, age 18 or higher, GPA 3.0 or higher, high school diploma, ability to obtain security clearance.
Awarded rate out of received applications: 11%
Degree type: Pursuing a regionally accredited undergraduate or graduate degree in: Aeronautical and Astronautical Engineering, Biosciences, Chemical Engineering, Chemistry, Civil Engineering, Cognitive, Neural, and Behavioral Sciences, Computer and Computational Sciences, Electrical Engineering, Geosciences, Industrial and Systems Engineering, Information Sciences, Materials Science and Engineering, Mathematics, Mechanical Engineering, Naval Architecture and Ocean Engineering, Nuclear Engineering, Oceanography, Operations Research, and Physics.
What's free? 100% tuition, yearly cash stipend of $25,000 to $38,000 (depending on major), health insurance allowance, and job placement with Department of Defense after graduation.
What's not? Living expenses
Service requirement: Each student must participate in an annual summer internship through college, and fill a 1 to 1 service contract upon graduation. For every 1 year of scholarship, 1 year of service is required.

COMPUTER SCIENCE or COMPUTER and ELECTRICAL ENGINEERING

Program Website:
https://www.nsa.gov/careers/jobs_search_apply/index.shtml
Program Title: Stokes Educational Scholarship Program (formerly Undergraduate Training Program)
Funding Source: National Security Agency
Eligibility: High school senior at the time of application, United States citizen, age 18 or higher, GPA 3.0 or higher, ability to obtain security clearance, a minimum SAT/College Board score of 1600 (1100 Critical Reading and Math, 500 in Writing) or ACT of 25
Awarded rate out of received applications: 20 awards annually. Average application cycle: 800 (2.5%)
Degree type: Regionally accredited bachelor's degree in Computer Science or Computer and Electrical Engineering.
What's free? $30,000 toward tuition, travel expenses and housing for summer internship, full time salary and benefits at the G4-1 rate during college, guaranteed employment with NSA after graduation, health and life insurance, and paid holidays.
What's not? Living expenses
Service requirement: Each student must participate in an annual 10 week summer internship through college, and fill a 1 to 1 service contract upon graduation. For every 1 year of scholarship, 1 year of service is required

CYBERSECURITY and INFORMATION ASSURANCE

Program Website: https://www.sfs.opm.gov
Program Title: CyberCorps Scholarship for Service
Funding Source: National Science Foundation and Department of Homeland Security
Eligibility: Must be a full-time student within two years of graduation with a bachelor's or master's degree; a student within three years of graduation with both the bachelor's and the master's degree; a student participating in a combined bachelor's and master's degree ("five year") program; or a research-based doctoral student within three years of graduation in a coherent formal academic program that is focused on cybersecurity or information assurance at an awardee institution; be a United States citizen; meet criteria for Federal employment; and be able to obtain a security clearance, if required.
Awarded rate out of received applications: 25-50%
Degree type: Bachelors or Master's degree.
What's free? 100% tuition, yearly cash stipend of $20,000 for undergraduates and $32,000 for graduate students, health insurance allowance, and books. This is a 2-year award.
What's not? Living expenses
Service requirement: Each student must participate in a summer internship while enrolled. Recipient must fill a 1 to 1 service contract upon graduation. For every 1 year of scholarship, 1 year of service at full pay is required. Rate of pay for bachelor's degree holders is GS7, for master's degree holders is GS9.

NURSING

Program Website: www.hrsa.gov
Program Title: NURSE Corps Scholarship Program
Funding Source: U.S. Department of Health and Human Services, Health Resources and Services Administration
Eligibility: U.S. Citizen, accepted for enrollment, not delinquent on student loan debt.
Awarded rate out of received applications: 225 awards will be given, but the rate is undisclosed. Considered competitive.
Degree type: Diploma leading to RN, Associate Degree of Nursing, Bachelors of Science Nursing, Masters of Science in Nursing, MSN-Nurse Practitioner, bridge programs.
What's free? 100% tuition, $1316 stipend per month, fees, books, clinical supplies, uniforms, and reasonable educational costs.
What's not? Living expenses
Service requirement: 2 years of service for scholarship in any amount. Additional years of service filled at a rate of 1 to 1 for scholarships longer than 2 years in a Critical Shortage Facility.

MEDICINE, PHYSICIAN ASSISTANT, DENTISTRY, CERTIFIED NURSE-MIDWIFE, or DOCTOR OF NURSING PRACTICE

Program Website: www.nhsc.hrsa.gov/scholarships
Program Title: National Health Services Corps
Funding Source:
Eligibility: U.S. Citizen, accepted for enrollment or current full time student.
Awarded rate out of received applications: 330 awards will be given, but the rate is undisclosed. Considered competitive.
Degree type: D.O., M.D., D.D.S., D.M.D., MSN-NP, MSN (CNM), P.A.
What's free? 100% tuition, $1316 stipend per month, fees, books, clinical supplies, uniforms, and reasonable educational costs. Scholars may also be eligible for undergraduate loan forgiveness after they have completed their scholarship service obligation.
What's not? tuition for repeated or failed coursework
Service requirement: 1-year service commitment per scholarship year or partial scholarship year; 2-year minimum and 4-year maximum in a Health Professionals Shortage Area.

TRADE OCCUPATIONS
Community College Trade Occupation Grants

Since March 2010, 4 years of funding have made their way into all 50 states' community college trade programs. President Obama's program, called Trade Adjustment Assistance Community College and Career Training Grant Program (TAACCCT), has spent somewhere in the neighborhood of 2 billion dollars to "expand and improve the ability to deliver education and career training programs that can be completed in two years or less." The grant program works in conjunction with each state's Department of Education and Department of Labor to identify and funnel dollars into the appropriate programs.

800 community colleges across every state have received grant dollars. For perspective, there are 1,132 community colleges in the United States, so approximately 70% of all community colleges. The U.S. Labor Secretary is asking for a 5th year of funding (2016), but no extension has been announced. Each college determines how to best use these funds. In many cases, new programs are being developed, but a few colleges are using these funds to waive tuition for students choosing certain programs. Since this program has technically ended, it is only a matter of time before each college's grant dollars are spent. As such, these programs may appear and vanish in as little as 1 semester. Be sure to search your local community college for current TAACCCT programs.

The following programs are currently funded through TAACCT, and representative of what you may find at your local community college:

County College of Morris
214 Center Grove Rd, Randolph, NJ 07869
(973) 328-5000
http://www.ccm.edu
What's free? 100% tuition for any certificate under the Health Professions Pathway Grant Program (Certified Nursing Assistant, Certified Homemaker Health Aide, Certified Medication Aide, Certified Medical Billing and Coding Specialist, Emergency Medical Technician (EMT), Clinical Medical Assistant (CMA), Phlebotomy Technician, EKG Technician, Certified Assisted Living Administrator, Pharmacy Technician, Dental Radiographic Technician, and Certified Alcohol and Drug Counselor), Transportation, books, uniforms, license fees, and childcare is also provided.
What's not? living expenses
Eligibility: GED or high school diploma, income criteria.

Jefferson College
1000 Viking Drive, Hillsboro, MO 63050
(636) 789-3000
www.jeffco.edu
What's free? 1 year Fast Track Electronics Technology Certificate (for immediate employment, but will transfer to a degree)
What's not? living expenses and books

New Hampshire Community College System (all 7 colleges)
www.ccsnh.edu
www.ampednh.com
What's free? Applied Career Fundamentals for Advanced Manufacturing Certificate (for immediate employment, but will transfer into an associate's degree)
What's not? living expenses and books
Eligibility: The NHCC system will fund 2000 full tuition grants distributed across all 7 colleges.

11 LOAN FORGIVENESS PROGRAMS

"Never spend your money before you have earned it."
-Thomas Jefferson

In my estimation, a motivated and resourceful student can earn a college degree without acquiring student loan debt. But what if you've found this book too late, and you've already accumulated student loan debt? Loan forgiveness programs may be worth considering as long as you're not already in default. Loan forgiveness programs are not a golden ticket, and require a tremendous commitment from the borrower in return for participation. In every case, you'll be obligated to a service contract for a set number of years in exchange for loan forgiveness.

Use caution, and read all of the fine print. Some programs only repay a small portion of your loans. Entering into a loan forgiveness program gives up your freedom to change jobs, relocate, take leave to have a baby, and a number of other constraints that you must consider.

FEDERAL PERKINS LOAN CANCELLATION PROGRAM
Website: https://studentaid.ed.gov
Summary: Eligible professions may qualify for up to 100% of
Federal Perkins Loan (Perkins Loan) cancellation.
Eligibility: Full-time firefighter, full-time law enforcement or
corrections officer, full-time nurse or medical technician, librarian,
full-time attorney employed in federal public or community defender
organization, full-time employee of a public child or family services
agency for high risk children, full-time staff member in a
prekindergarten or child care program licensed by the state, speech
pathologist, special education teacher, or faculty member at a tribal
college.
To apply: Contact the financial aid office of the school you
attended when you took out the loan

FEDERAL PUBLIC SERVICE LOAN FORGIVENESS
Website: https://studentaid.ed.gov
Summary: If you work full time (30 hours + per week) for a
qualifying public service organization (federal, state, or local
government agency, entity, or organization or a not-for-profit
organization) the balance of your loans you received under the
William D. Ford Federal Direct Loan (Direct Loan) Program are
eligible for Public Service Loan Forgiveness after 10 years of on-time
payments.
Eligibility: You must make 120 on-time, full, scheduled, monthly
payments on your Direct Loans under a qualified repayment plan. (10
years) When you make each of those payments, you must be
working full-time at a qualifying public service organization. Lump
sum payments or payments you make as advance payments for future
months are not qualifying payments. Loans you received under the
Federal Family Education Loan (FFEL) Program, the Federal Perkins
Loan (Perkins Loan) Program, or any other student loan program are
not eligible for PSLF.
To apply: Contact Federal Loan Servicing. www.myfedloan.org

FEDERAL TEACHER LOAN FORGIVENESS

Website: https://studentaid.ed.gov

Summary: Teachers employed for 5 consecutive years at an elementary or secondary school in which more than 30% of the students qualified for services under Title I, may receive $17,500

Eligibility: Eligibility and forgiveness are very specific to each teacher's credential and experience. See website.

To apply: Complete the application
http://ifap.ed.gov/dpcletters/attachments/GEN1419AttachTeacher
LoanForgivenessApp.pdf

MILITARY ENLISTMENT INCENTIVE
Student Loan Repayment

Eligibility: Be aware that receiving loan repayment incentives may require relinquishing future G.I. Bill benefits.

To apply: Contact your branch's recruitment office.

Air Force: www.af.mil
Enlistment Incentive: Up to $10,000 of qualifying student loans

Army: www.army.mil
Enlistment Incentive: Up to $65,000 of qualifying student loans

Navy: www.navy.mil
Enlistment Incentive: Up to $65,000 of qualifying student loans

12 EMPLOYER TUITION REIMBURSEMENT

"You're not a bad parent if you don't save for your kid's college because instead you had to choose to feed them and clothe them. Those things come first. They can go to school and do this thing called 'work' while they're in school."
-Dave Ramsey

The Society for Human Resource Management is the largest human resource management organization in the world. In their 2014 Employee Benefits Research Report, only 9% of companies reduced their employee educational benefits, while 91% *increased* or maintained these benefits they extended to their employees.

Companies see the benefits of offering tuition reimbursement and tuition assistance to their employees. According to the report, 54% of all employers offered undergraduate tuition assistance, and 50% offered graduate level tuition assistance.

Tuition assistance programs can pay for part or all of your degree. Each company that creates a program will attach strings, which require careful consideration. Common strings include holding full time employment, pursuing a specific major, maintain passing grades, and so on. The human resources department at any company can provide detailed information about their program.

Companies that offer 100% TUITION REIMBURSEMENT

Aeropostale	Ann Taylor	Applied Materials
Apple	AT&T	Bank of America
Barnes & Noble	Best Buy	Boeing
BP	Capital One	CarMax
Chase Bank	Chevron	Comerica Bank
Cobham Missions	Coca-Cola	Deloitte
Discover Card	Disney	ExxonMobil
FedEx	Ford	Gap
General Electric	Google	Harris Teeter
Hilton Hotels	Home Depot	IBM
Intel	Iowa Health Systems	J.M. Smucker Co.
John Deere	Johnson & Johnson	KFC Restaurants
Kohl's	Lane Bryant	Macy's
Marriott Corp.	McDonald's	Nike
Proctor & Gamble	Publix Grocery	Raytheon
Sheetz	Siemens	Staples
Starbucks	Target	UPS
Verizon Wireless	Walgreens (pharmacy school only)	
Walmart	Wells Fargo	Yahoo

If your employer provides 100% tuition assistance, and isn't on this list, I want to hear about it!
Send me a message at CompletelyFREEColleges@aol.com

APPENDICES

APPENDIX I
Jennifer's 10 Favorite Websites

1.   www.Facebook.com/CompletelyFREEColleges
Completely FREE College's Facebook page. It's my book's official fan page. Updates to this book's content shared daily.

2.   www.collegeboard.org
The College Board's official page for everything related to AP, SAT, and CLEP test information. Use their site to research test prep material and schedule your exams.

3.   ope.ed.gov/accreditation
Department of Education's Accreditation database. You can look up any college's official accreditation information. It's the database I used to research this book.

4.   www.degreeinfo.com
Degree Info is my favorite distance learning forum. If you're considering distance learning, this is the best place to start. If you visit, say hello, my username over there is Cookderosa.

5.   www.degreeforum.net
If you'd like to test out of a degree, Degree Forum is the best resource. I tested out of 2 degrees (not my first one or my last one, but the two in the middle). I dedicated my first book, Homeschooling for College Credit, to the members of that forum. If you visit, say hello, my username over there is Cookderosa.

6.   www.Saylor.org

My favorite free learning resource –ever! While you can't earn a free degree through Saylor, you can get as much learning as your brain can handle. They've recently arranged college credit-earning options for many of their free classes! If you're unsure about taking a class in college, you can try it out first over at Saylor.

7.   www.bls.gov/ooh

The Department of Labor's Occupational Outlook Handbook is my "go-to" for any and all occupational research. If you're a young person considering a career, or an adult considering a change, check out the online handbook. It's fantastic! Don't pick a career without a visit.

8.   www.hslda.org

If you're considering homeschooling, Home School Legal Defense Association provides a legal summary for each state, and helps you comply with those laws. They also have a huge listing of support groups. My family has homeschooled since 1994 and been members just as long.

9.   www.daveramsey.com

Before taking out a student loan, get a daily dose of Dave. He'll set you straight. He inspired my family to live a debt-free lifestyle, which led me to wonder if free college was possible? Yes!

10. www.Gladwell.com

Malcolm Gladwell is my favorite smart person, I devour everything he writes.

APPENDIX II

You're overpaying for college if you...

1. **Attend an out of state public college.** You're paying double $ for a degree available in your back yard. You also make yourself ineligible for in-state scholarships.
2. **Were enticed by the "freshman scholarship."** A lot of the time, scholarships are just marketing tools to drive enrollment. Calculate the degree's total tuition for four years, not just one year. Subtract the scholarship amount (do it for each year if it is reoccurring) and use that number to compare costs.
3. **Attend a "not top 100" private liberal arts college.** These colleges come with a "top 100" price tag but little to no brand-recognition.
4. **Choose a major with low return on investment.** If you're going to follow your passion, be sure you can pay cash for the whole degree. If you're taking on a quarter million dollars of debt, be sure you can get a job.
5. **Make brand assumptions.** There are 23,700 regionally accredited colleges and universities in the United States. Most people don't know one from the next, but most people think *everyone else* knows them all. They don't. If you're fortunate enough to graduate from any accredited college, you'll be in the top 1/3 of Americans by educational attainment; brand doesn't matter.

Jennifer Cook - DeRosa

APPENDIX III

College Majors and
Return on Investment

Georgetown University's Center on Education and Workforce analyzed the economic value of 171 college majors. The median earnings between majors varied as much as 300%! This report suggests *what* you study is much more important than *where* you study.

10 Highest Median Earnings by Major
Petroleum Engineer ($120,000)
Pharmacy/pharmaceutical Sciences ($105,000)
Mathematics and Computer Sciences ($98,000)
Aerospace Engineering ($87,000)
Chemical Engineering ($86,000)
Electrical Engineering ($85,000)
Naval Architecture and Marine Engineering ($82,000)
Mechanical Engineering ($80,000)
Metallurgical Engineering ($80,000)
Mining/ Mineral Engineering ($80,000)

10 Lowest Median Earnings by Major
Counseling/Psychology ($29,000)
Early Childhood Education ($36,000)
Theology and Religious Vocations ($38,000)
Human Services and Community Organizations ($38,000)
Social Work ($39,000)
Drama and Theater, Studio Arts, Communication ($40,000)
Disorders Sciences and Services, ($40,000)
Visual and Performing Arts ($40,000)
Health and Medical Preparatory Programs ($40,000)

1Jennifer Cook - DeRosa

APPENDIX IV

College Coach for Parents

1. If your child is younger than 9th grade

Turn to chapter 3. If you live near a town with a Promise program, consider relocating into a Promise district if you have more than 1 child. The value of a Promise program relocation can range from $5,000 to $200,000 per child. If no programs exist, read chapter 5.

2. If your child is still in high school

Read chapters 5 and chapter 6. If your child is 1 or more years away from graduation, consider employment with one of the 600+ Scholarship Exchange schools. The value of a job change can range from $30,000 to $120,000 per child. If your child is already in 11th or 12th grade, take full advantage of free dual enrollment opportunities in your state.

3. If your child has already started 12th grade

Fill out the Free FAFSA application to see if your child qualifies for a Pell Grant. Eligibility is determined automatically when you complete the form. Read chapter 4 regarding income thresholds. Read chapters 2, 8, 9, 10, and 12.

4. If your child has already graduated from High School, but is under age 21

Consider all colleges in chapters 2 and 9. Consider military enlistment or ROTC options in chapter 8, or scholarship career paths in chapter 10. Finally, consider working full time for one of the companies in chapter 12.

Contact Jennifer Cook-DeRosa

Email: CompletelyFREEColleges@aol.com

Jennifer's Facebook pages and groups:

Completely FREE Colleges page
www.Facebook.com/CompletelyFREEColleges

Homeschooling for College Credit page
www.Facebook.com/HomeschoolingforCollegeCredit

Homeschooling in North Carolina group
www.Facebook.com/groups/NCHS4CC

Twitter:
@cookderosa for Completely FREE Colleges
@JDExplainsIt for Homeschooling for College Credit

YouTube Channel: Homeschooling for College Credit

Jennifer Cook - DeRosa

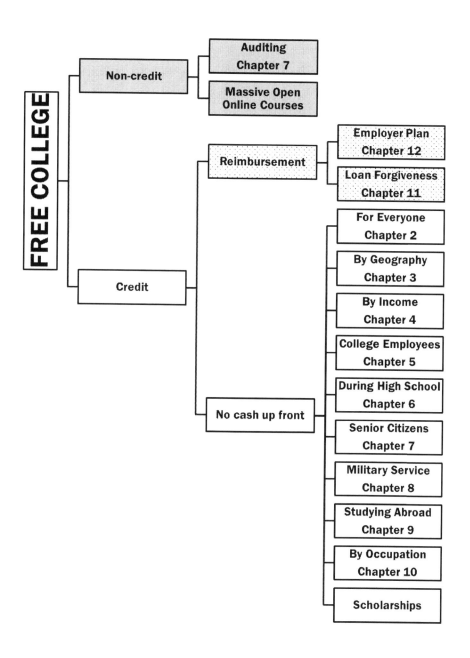

INDEX of COLLEGES

Florida International University · 130
Florida Southern College · 75
Florida State University · 130
Fontbonne University · 91
Fordham University · 96
Franklin & Marshall College · 105
Franklin College · 80
Franklin Pierce University · 93
Franklin University · 101
Franklin W. Olin College of
   Engineering · 21
Freie Universitat Berlin · 180
Fresno Pacific University · 71
Friends University · 83
Furman University · 110, 138

G

Galesburg Promise Program · 33
Gannon University · 105
Gardner-Webb University · 99
Garrett College · 36
Garrett County Scholarship Program
   · 36
Geneva College · 106
George Fox University · 104
George Washington University · 74
Georgetown College · 83
Georgian Court University · 94
Gettysburg College · 106
Goddard College · 114
Gonzaga University · 117
Goodwin College · 73
Goucher College · 85
Graceland University · 82
Grand Canyon University · 69
Grand View University · 82
Granite State College · 135
Green Mountain College · 115
Greensboro College · 99
Grove City College · 106
Guilford College · 99
Gustavus Adolphus College · 89
Gwynedd Mercy University · 106

H

Haaga-Helia University of Applied
   Sciences · 176
Hamline University · 89
Hammond College Bound Program ·
   34
Hampden-Sydney College · 116
Hampshire College · 86
Hanover College · 80
Harding University · 70
Hardin-Simmons University · 112
Hartwick College · 96
Harvard University · 58
Hastings College · 92
Hazel Park Promise Program · 38
Heidelberg University · 101, 181
Hellenic College Holy Cross · 87
Helsinki Metropolia University of
   Applied Sciences · 177
Hendrix College · 70
Heritage University · 117
High Point University · 99
Hilbert College · 96
Hillsdale College · 88
Hiram College · 101
Hobart and William Smith Colleges ·
   96
Hochschule Worms University of
   Applied Sciences · 181
Hofstra University · 96
Hollins University · 116
Holy Cross College · 80
Holy Family University · 106
Hood College · 85
Hopkinsville Community College · 36
Hopkinsville Rotary Scholars
   Program · 36
Houghton College · 96
Houston Baptist University · 113
Howard Payne University · 113
Humboldt State University · 128
Huntingdon College · 69
Huntington University · 80

Lynn University · 75
Lyon College · 70

M

Macaulay Honors College at City
  University of New York · 42
MacMurray College · 78
Macromedia University of Applied
  Sciences for Media and
  Communication · 182
Madonna University · 88
Maine College of Art · 84
Mainz University · 182
Malone University · 102
Manchester University · 80
Manhattan College · 96
Manhattanville College · 96
Marian University · 80, 118
Marietta College · 102
Marlboro College · 115
Mars Hill University · 100
Martinsburg College · 47
Mary Baldwin College · 116
Marygrove College · 88
Maryland Institute College of Art · 85
Marylhurst University · 104
Marymount California University · 71
Marymount University · 116
Maryville College · 111
Maryville University · 91
Marywood University · 106
Massachusetts Institute of
  Technology (MIT) · 59
McDaniel College · 85
McKendree University · 78
McMurry University · 113
Medaille College · 97
Memphis College of Art · 112
Mercer University · 76
Mercy College · 82, 97, 102
Mercy College of Health Sciences ·
  82
Mercyhurst University · 107
Meredith College · 100

Merrimack College · 87
Methodist College · 78, 93, 111
Methodist University · 100
Michigan college · 37, 40
Michigan State University · 39
Mid-Atlantic Christian University ·
  100
Midway College · 84
Mikkeli University of Applied
  Sciences · 178
Milligan College · 112
Millikin University · 78
Mills College · 71
Millsaps College · 90
Minneapolis College of Art & Design
  · 89
Misericordia University · 107
Mississippi College · 90
Mississippi County Great River
  Promise · 31
Missouri Baptist University · 91
Mitchell College · 73, 90
Molloy College · 97
Monmouth College · 78
Monmouth University · 94
Moore College of Art and Design ·
  107
Moravian College · 107
Morningside College · 82
Mount Aloysius College · 107
Mount Holyoke College · 87
Mount Ida College · 87
Mount Marty College · 111
Mount Mercy University · 82
Mount Saint Mary College · 97
Mount Saint Mary's University · 71
Mount St. Joseph University · 102
Mount St. Mary's University · 85
Mount Vernon Nazarene University ·
  102
Muhlenberg College · 107
Muskingum University · 102

Presbyterian College · 110
Prescott College · 69
Princeton Theological Seminary · 107
Princeton University · 60
Providence College · 109

Q

Queens University of Charlotte · 100
Quincy University · 79
Quinnipiac University · 73

R

Randolph College · 116
Randolph-Macon College · 116
Reformed Theological Seminary · 90
Regent University · 116
Regis College · 87
Regis University · 72
Rhine-Waal University of Applied
   Sciences · 183
Richmond Promise · 32
Rider University · 94
Ripon College · 118
Roanoke College · 116
Robert Morris University · 79, 107
Rochester Institute of Technology ·
   97, 136
Rockford University · 79
Rockhurst University · 91
Rocky Mountain College · 92
Roger Williams University · 109
Rollins College · 75
Roosevelt University, · 79
Rose-Hulman Institute of
   Technology · 80
Rosemont College · 107
Rusk Tyler Junior College Citizens
   Promise · 46
Rutgers University · 135

S

Sacred Heart University · 73
Sage College · 98
Saginaw Promise Program · 41
Saginaw Valley State University · 133
Saint Anselm College · 93
Saint Francis University · 108
Saint John's University College of St.
   Benedict · 89
Saint Joseph's College · 80, 84
Saint Joseph's University · 108
Saint Leo University · 75, 156
Saint Louis University · 91
Saint Martin's University · 117
Saint Mary-of-the-Woods College · 80
Saint Mary's College of California ·
   71
Saint Mary's University · 90
Saint Michael's College · 115
Saint Peter's University · 94
Saint Vincent College · 108
Saint Xavier University, · 79
Salem Academy & College · 100
Salve Regina University · 109
Samford University · 69
San Diego State University · 128
San Francisco State University · 128
Santa Clara University · 71, 128
Sarah Lawrence College · 98
Say Yes Buffalo Program · 43
Say Yes Syracuse Program · 43
School of the Art Institute of Chicago
   · 79
Schreiner University · 113
Seattle University · 117
Seton Hall University · 94
Seton Hill University · 108
Sharjah · 114
Shenandoah University · 116
Shorter University · 76
Sierra College · 128
Sierra Nevada College · 93
Simmons College · 87
Simpson College · 82

U

Made in the USA
San Bernardino, CA
01 December 2015